An Introduction to Operational Risk

An Introduction to Operational Risk

By Thomas Kaiser and Marc Köhne

Riskbooks

Published by Risk Books, a Division of Incisive Financial Publishing Ltd

Haymarket House
28–29 Haymarket
London SW1Y 4RX
Tel: +44 (0)20 7484 9700
Fax: +44 (0)20 7484 9800
E-mail: books@incisivemedia.com
Sites: www.riskbooks.com
www.incisivemedia.com

ISBN 1 904339 51 4

British Library Cataloguing in Publication Data
A catalogue record for this book is available from the British Library

Publisher: Laurie Donaldson
Assistant Editor: Jennifer Gibb
Designer: Rebecca Bramwell

Typeset by Mizpah Publishing Services Private Limited, Chennai, India

Printed and bound in Spain by Espacegrafic, Pamplona, Navarra

Updated translation of the German book: Operationelle Risiken in Finanzinstituten, Gabler Verlang, Wiesbaden 2004

Contents

List of Figures

List of Tables

About the Authors

Dr Thomas Kaiser is a director with KPMG Germany in the Financial Risk Management area and heads its Operational Risk practice. In addition, he is a lecturer on operational risk at Frankfurt University. Before joining KPMG, he worked in the risk management departments of three major German banks, focusing on operational risk.

Marc Felix Köhne is a partner with KPMG Germany in the Management Assurance Services area. He is responsible for the Global Operational Risk competence team. Before joining KPMG, he worked in derivates trading as well as operational risk management with a major German bank.

Preface

A growing demand on the part of practitioners and academics for comprehensive treatments of operational risk have prompted us to commit to paper our many years of – partly joint – experience gained in banks and in banking consultancy in the form of this book. Our aim is to provide a survey of the current state of this discipline, important unsettled issues and approaches to solutions to the comprehensive management and control of operational risks. Since best practices have not yet emerged throughout all areas or are very likely to develop further, this project must restrict itself to the main approaches, without being able to rule out the possibility of new ideas leading to shifts in future approaches to this topic.

The publishing date was chosen to enable us to take into account the contents and implications of the new Capital Accord of the Basel Committee on Banking Supervision (Basel II), as well as the EU Commission's Capital Requirements Directive (CRD).

This book would not have been possible without the direct and indirect factual and moral support of the operational risk community. Our special thanks are due to our wives for their repeated critical and constructive proofreading of the work and in particular for their time, which can hardly be counted as family life. Further thanks are also due to all who have contributed to a significant number of discussions in projects, seminars and publications. Last but not least, many thanks to Peter de Groot in the Netherlands, who was instrumental in the initial translation of the German original version of this book.

All of this, in one form or another, has contributed to the book. Any remaining errors remain, of course, the sole responsibility of the authors.

We hope this work will be of use in implementing appropriate processes and methods at financial institutions and will also support the urgently needed, broader reception of the topic in academic discussion.

Thomas Kaiser
Marc Felix Köhne
Steinbach (Taunus) and Munich, September 2006

1 Introduction

Substantial losses (including Barings, Orange County and, more recently, Allied Irish Bank) have drawn attention to the area of "operational risk" (not always synonymous with "operating risks" or "operative risks", and frequently referred to in short as "Op Risk"). This interest has emerged both within financial institutions and the banking supervisory authorities since the mid-1990s (see eg, Risk Books, 1998; BBA/ISDA/RMA, 1999). It has led to the institutionalisation of a discipline that has already been established for some decades in other business sectors such as manufacturing, military, aerospace and nuclear safety. Of course, the financial industry has been facing operational risks implicitly and explicitly as long as it has existed, and will continue to do so. However, this has not happened within a dedicated, consistent and comprehensive methodological framework. Since operational risk has several definitions, in what follows (unless explicitly stated otherwise) it will be defined as the "risk of loss resulting from inadequate or failed internal processes, people and systems or from external events", thus following the definition resulting from the Basel II consultation process.

The aim of this book is to offer a framework for managing operational risk as it can be observed in various stages of design and implementation by leading international banks, both early adopters and fast followers. Common structural elements – as well as differences in the methods used – will be described. One main focus will be on providing pragmatic approaches to solving the manifold problems that will inevitably occur when designing and implementing such a framework. However, it should be kept in mind here that – due to the relatively short period of intensive work on this topic within the industry, especially compared with areas such as credit and market risk – many approaches are still in a preliminary or incubator phase, and that generally accepted best practices have not yet emerged, and in some areas probably never will.

In addition to the business-driven motivation to manage operational risks, the relevant regulatory requirements (publication of the Basel Committee on Banking Supervision, "Basel II", June 2004, and the EU Commission's Capital Requirements Directive, "CRD", June 2006) will be presented and analysed in some detail.

This book is intended not only to support finance industry experts who have been entrusted with this problem in the implementing of appropriate projects. It also aims at stimulating academic discussion of the problems posed by operational risk management. As a result of the links between operational risk management and human behaviour, organisational considerations and so forth, a variety of starting points for interdisciplinary research may be found here.

2

Drivers for Operational Risk Management

A variety of reasons have induced financial institutions, in particular banks and now more and more insurance companies, to show intense interest in the topic of operational risk management. As is true in many cases, two main drivers can be observed: on the one hand, economic or business reasons for managing this risk in a better way; and, on the other hand, regulatory requirements forcing the more hesitatant institutions to address the issue, too. Whereas the first banks which, 10 years ago, made initial steps towards establishing the subject within their risk management, were exclusively driven by economic considerations (mainly significant loss events), for the majority of banks it became a pressing topic only with the publication of the first Basel Consultation Paper in 1999. That regulatory requirements will have to be fulfilled is indisputable. The risk of non-compliance will almost always lead to an increase in regulatory capital, resulting in higher capital costs, and, as the ultimate threat, lead up to the termination of business operations. Nevertheless, any such far-reaching changes to a bank's risk management, with repercussions in all areas, also need to be supported by business considerations to become meaningful and provide real business benefits, which can clearly be observed in the current discussion of the Sarbanes–Oxley Act and its cost and benefit implications. To justify the implementation of a comprehensive framework for the management of operational risk, purely to comply with regulatory requirements would result in failing to take advantage of its full potential. Nevertheless, it is always difficult to

Figure 1 The benefits of managing operational risk

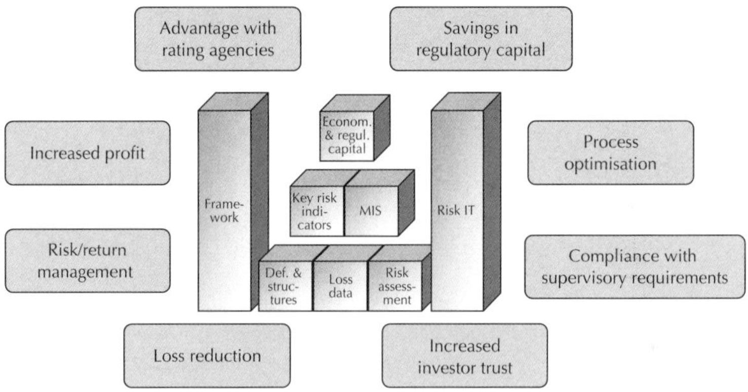

justify the improvement of risk management with economic reasons, due to the perceived cost character of these changes, whereas the regulatory angle can almost never be ignored. In the following, this book attempts to present both drivers and the conceptual framework to address them.

BUSINESS DRIVERS

To derive the drivers for operational risk management, it may be worth defining risk management as such. Since it consists of two terms, *risk* and *management*, an analytical approach would be, first, to decompose these two terms, define them separately and then derive a definition of risk management from this.

Since the introduction of modern portfolio theory, risk has been seen as a deviation from an expected value. This, theoretically – and frequently contrary to public opinion – includes both positive and negative deviations. In practice there is a tendency to tolerate a positive deviation as being desirable, or at least acceptable, whereas a negative deviation is very frequently considered the main subject of risk management. For this book, the portfolio theory's view of risk as a positive or negative deviation will be adopted, although, in the area of operational risk, it may be even harder to see the positive aspect of an event.

As for management, it should basically be defined as goal-oriented (or rational) economic behaviour.

Figure 2 Portfolio theory

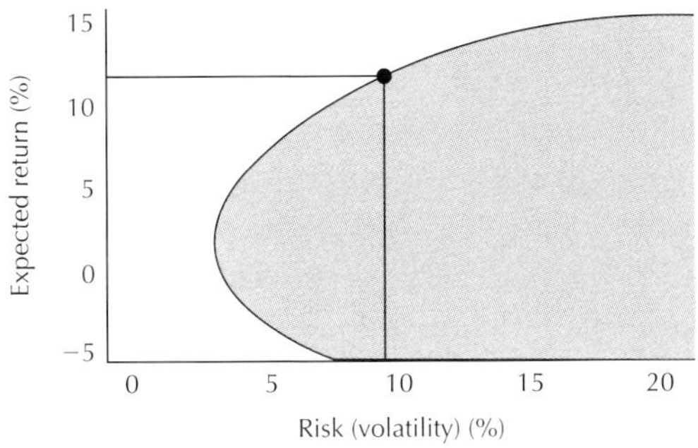

Risk management can accordingly be seen as exerting a rational influence on risks. This includes, in addition to taking and accepting risks, variations such as reducing, transferring and completely eliminating them. Rational behaviour supposes that risks are accepted only when they are matched by an expected adequate reward. Modern portfolio theory has refined this statement to the extent that this is deemed rational only when no higher expected reward can be obtained elsewhere in return for accepting a given unit of risk, or the expected reward cannot be obtained with less risk (see Markowitz 1952). Since economic action can be defined as the allocation of scarce resources and since, in reality, nearly every decision involves uncertainty, as a conclusion, every economic decision implies taking more or less risk. If action necessarily involves uncertainty, then it is accompanied by certain expectations regarding the expected rewards. Portfolio theory has operationalised this line of thought by defining this expectation of reward as expected return, and the risk of deviating from this return as volatility – ie, the fluctuation margin either side of this expected return. Therefore upside and downside deviations are possible. Obviously, the greater the risk, the higher the expected return should be.

Moreover, market participants act rationally only when they enter into a transaction that promises the highest expected return with the same risk, or the lowest risk for the same level of return. Any deviation from this, expressed as a risk–reward ratio that does not lie on the line of efficiency, does not reflect rational behaviour and will not be rewarded appropriately.

For market and credit risks, this connection is obvious and generally accepted, although by no means trivial. In the case of operational risk the connection is significantly more complex. This is the result of the considerable lack of clarity regarding scope, definition and boundaries of operational risk that still prevails. There has been a growing consensus in the past as to what is to be understood by the concept, and whether operational risk can be identified and measured. There remains, however, a lot of uncertainty regarding the "how to" and some members of the community remain extremely critical today. It therefore, not surprisingly, was and still is difficult to assign management activities to this risk.

Only in recent times can a change in this perception be observed, at least in the financial sector. The main causes of this are:

- the growing notion that an organisation's control framework is complete only when it covers all risk components (ie, it is not restricted to market and credit risk);
- the growing perception of operational risk as a distinct type of risk on the same level as market and credit risk, and the development of a generally accepted definition and the growing consistency in the management approaches;
- the resulting accelerated development of methods and techniques for the consistent identification, measurement, management and monitoring of operational risk and the allocation of specific resources;
- the availability of specific software to support the process of managing operational risk; and
- the availability of adequate human resources.

Due to the remaining heterogeneity of the components or categories subsumed under operational risk, it does, however, remain difficult to construct a risk–reward relationship similar to other risk types.

One major difficulty is caused by the tendency to define operational risk solely in negative terms – to exclude positive deviation *a priori* and therefore not consider it a deviation from an expected outcome regardless of the deviations direction. This results in an inconsistent treatment of this risk. This is based on the premise that all elements of an operation "work" almost without error in a defined standard state; in other words, the risk results only in a diminished performance and/or an increased error rate.

Even if this perception is apparently correct for some elements – at least on superficial consideration – it can be considered doubtful whether this view can be generalised and whether it should have fundamental significance for all operational risk components and for their conceptual treatment.

Example 1

At first glance, it may be difficult to find a suitable example of such a connection in a building fire. The occurrence is generally considered as highly undesirable and thus as a clearly negative deviation from an expected value or outcome. However, if the scope of the consideration is extended to all prior and subsequent management actions and all costs associated therewith, this results in a different picture. The costs of the fire occurring are weighed against the costs of insurance, fire detection and alarm systems, and of running costs for a replacement site and all other costs associated with this scenario. The value of the expected outcome thus changes from the non-occurrence to a result in which the actual costs of insurance premiums and other risk measures are weighed against the costs of occurrence times its probability. Thus, the possibility of a positive or a negative deviation from the expected value can arise in both cases, the event or non-event, if the running costs of all risk-mitigating efforts deviate from the expected (predicted) loss weighted by its probability or, in the case of an event, from the actual loss. Action would be irrational if this relationship were not considered in the management process. It is thus possible, at a conceptual level at least, to establish consistency with the concept of risk management applied to other risk types for an example with a possible outcome, which is at first glance considered an entirely negative deviation.

Example 2

Another example can be constructed related to processing costs. The costs of processing quality depend to some extent on the costs of controls embedded in these processes. The decision to intensify or reduce such controls reflects the same risk–reward concept. Establishing additional or improved controls will very likely result in a reduction of the absolute number of losses from processing errors, or, in other words results in an entirely positive deviation from the former expected outcome. But in this case, too, all components, including the additional control costs, must be taken into consideration. The expected value is thus no longer just somehow lower than the current losses due to poor process quality, but should deviate from the previously expected value by exactly the additional control costs less the reduced losses due to processing errors. Of course, such controls would not be established if this connection were to result in higher overall costs, such as increased cost of control without any reduction in losses from processing errors. But in this case, too, the risk is that of a deviation from the new expected value. The reduced losses due to processing errors can deviate from the new expected overall costs of control in both directions.

The two examples show that operational risk can be defined as a positive or negative deviation from an expected value, just like other types of risk. Admittedly, the relevant expected value is in many cases less obvious than in the case of market or credit risks, as it does not consist of simply a targeted result but has to be determined taking into account actual or opportunity costs. Management therefore needs to take all relevant components into account and define a target result or expected outcome ie, derived from that. Practical implementation of this concept is, however, further complicated by the broad definition of operational risk. Even categories or subcategories are in many cases too heterogeneous for such a risk–reward consideration. In most cases, the parameters needed for the complete picture can be obtained for only smaller, well-defined entities, such as products and processes.

Of course, the analysis of business drivers for operational risk management falls short of its aim if such a concept is designed only because it can be fitted into a theoretical model consistent with other independent risks. Managing operational risk makes sense independently of the theoretical consideration of a deviation from a hard-to-construct expected value, because it reduces risk and thus costs. Whether it can also increase the return is a question of perspective.

Other, more real world drivers for managing such risks currently include the increasingly more consistent considerations of process improvements through quality management, and the necessity of including insurance programmes, disaster recovery plans and business continuity management into a consistent overall risk management framework. The growing perception that sourcing relationships are in need of tighter control or better risk management is also developing as a significant driver. Of course, none of the trends above – with the exception of sourcing control – is in itself new.

What *is* new, however, is the treatment of these issues under the central headline of operational risk management. Whereas the cost side has almost always been taken into account in the past when implementing quality management measures, the risk perspective in many cases provides an entirely new and important angle. This especially applies to the areas of emergency and business continuity planning and insurance. Not only was their management in the past largely autonomous and often not sufficiently related to the individual business lines, but also the post mortem analysis of the effects and the implementation of measures was managed at the business unit level, so that only limited knowledge sharing could emerge and comparisons were difficult due to inconsistent ways of evaluating, aggregating and reporting. For example, only few business line managers know which aspects of their units, processes or products are covered by an insurance programme, and to what extent. This is very often deliberately done by insurance programme managers in order not to further moral hazard. But, as a consequence, a line manager may implement risk-mitigating measures to reduce risk that the insurance department has already taken care of in a different form. Outsourcing as such is an area of considerable operational risk, due to the trend of contracting out certain operations to emerging specialised transactions banks, eg, IT operations for divisions or entire banks. Often left with very limited control over the outsourcing provider and the resulting quality of service, the risks remain with the outsourcer, as all stakeholders will address him first in the case of shortcomings. Only in a second step may a reimbursement kick in, depending on the contractual terms agreed on. Consistent treatment of these significant aspects of operational risk will certainly lead to more positive results. By reducing the risks accepted, losses will be reduced immediately or over time, leading to an equivalent increase in profit.

Improved management of risks and returns can consequently be achieved, covering not only market and credit risks but also operational risk. Rating agencies are making it much clearer that the quality and extent of risk management as a whole, and therefore of its components – including operational risk management – can directly affect a bank's or insurer's rating. Assessments of the enterprise-wide risk management framework with all its components are increasingly becoming part of the rating process and thus have a direct effect on a financial institution's funding costs. This again is incorporated by other stakeholders into their pricing decisions as risk premiums to cover the specific risks involved in dealing with an entity that provides better- or worse-quality risk management.

Of course, given the present state of development of the concept, in particular the early stages of quantification methods, there is reason to doubt that the given nexus between loss reduction, improved risk–reward management and effects on ratings due to the quality of operational risk can easily be measured. However, these effects exist and, if not the magnitude, then the direction of their individual impacts is undisputed. It has to be conceded, nevertheless, that today this ratio can only in limited areas be exactly expressed in terms of risk and reward and whether an investment in better risk measures in the area of operational risk can be fully justified or not.

In the early 1990s, the idea that all of a bank's market risk-bearing positions could be aggregated into a single figure that expresses the risks taken was at best unknown to most market participants, if not considered totally unrealistic. This is all the more astonishing because the essential features of the theoretical basis existed as early as the 1950s. Similarly, many traditionally minded credit officers still find it relatively difficult to understand that a lending decision is not made on an individual basis entirely any more, but that, nowadays, overarching portfolio considerations are taken into account.

Similar considerations apply in today's efforts to establish a consistent framework for the management of operational risk. Even if certain elements – such as insurance programmes, quality management and emergency planning – require considerable expert knowledge, there remains the similar objective of measuring these risks in a consistent manner and forming an opinion on the quality of their management. Measuring the reduction of risk emanating from processes, people, systems and external events in order to assess the economic impact of a related investment is being placed on a better footing by operational risk management in a gradual process. Similarly, rating agencies are already refining their valuation methods, and internal and external stakeholders are including more than just the market and credit risk issues in their decisions.

REGULATORY ENVIRONMENT

Because of its broad spectrum, the topic of operational risk was initially broached indirectly by the supervisory authorities with publications on topics such as the internal control system and quality management. The Basel Committee on Banking Supervision (BCBS) addressed the subject explicitly for the first time in its publication (see BIS 1998) from a qualitative point of view.

Sound Practices

The first complete set of recommendations that concentrates on operational risk exclusively is the "Sound Practices for the Management and Supervision of Operational Risk" paper ("Sound Practices"), which was published by the Basel Committee on Banking Supervision in February 2003 (see BIS 2003a), based on two consultation papers dated December 2001 and July 2002.

"Sound Practices" makes recommendations concerning organisational responsibility and for structuring the content of the process of managing operational risk, including the supervisory review process and disclosure to market participants.

The organisational environment for operational risk management is defined in the first section of "Sound Practices". According to Principle 1, the Board of Management has the responsibility for the introduction and regular review of general conditions for managing operational risk as an independent discipline. According to Principle 2, the bank-wide framework defined therein must be regularly reviewed by an internal audit independent of risk management. Principle 3 points out management's responsibility for the consistent implementation of the framework throughout the entire bank. The various responsibilities in the risk management process must be communicated to all employees. The procedures must be

Figure 3 The "10 commandments" of operational risk sound practices

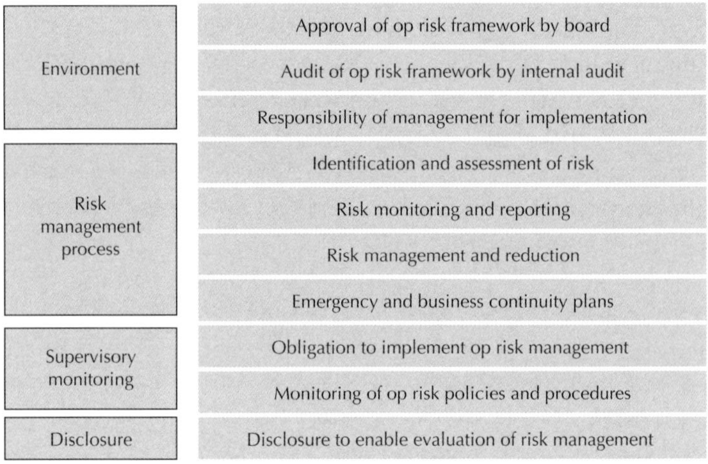

implemented in a structured form of principles, instructions and processes.

The second section details the components of the operational risk management process. Principle 4 requires the identification and assessment of operational risk for all major products, activities, processes and systems. Furthermore, it must be ensured that an assessment of the inherent operational risk be conducted before the introduction of new products, activities, processes or systems. Principle 5 prescribes the monitoring of the operational risk profile with special focus on material risks. The system of reporting to the Board of Management has to support a proactive operational risk management. Requirements on instruments for the mitigation and reduction of risk are reflected in Principle 6. Strategies for the limitation and mitigation of risks are to be examined and adjusted regularly in the light of the entire risk-taking capacity and risk profile. Lastly, Principle 7 requires emergency and business continuity plans limiting losses in the case of the occurrence of a significant event.

The role of the supervisory authorities is specified in the third section. Supervisors are, according to Principle 8, expected to require the existence of an effective framework for the operational risk management as a component of the whole management approach from all banks in their jurisdiction. Under Principle 9, supervisory bodies should carry out regular independent reviews of compliance with principles, instructions and processes related to the management of operational risk. A procedure for tracking relevant developments in banks must be guaranteed as well.

The role of disclosure is described in the last section. Market participants should be able to assess the approach to the operational risk management of a business partner on the basis of adequately disclosed of information.

History of the development of Basel II and CRD

Whereas "Sound Practices" has only the character of recommendations and is aimed at influencing individual supervisory bodies, Basel II and CRD provide binding rules for the treatment of operational risk. Their overriding purpose is to guarantee the functioning of the financial system as a prerequisite for the smooth operation of all other economic activity globally. They are less concerned in the stability of an individual financial institution. To achieve global financial stability, the adequacy of banks' capital is regulated, in order to provide a cushion against the occurrence of losses up to a certain degree. Until the introduction of Basel II and CRD, the Basel Capital Accord (Basel I) (see BIS 1988a) and the Brussels Capital Adequacy Directive (CAD 2) (see EC 1993) pose capital requirements only for credit and market risks.

The first consultation paper on the new Basel II Accord on the Adequacy of Banks' Capital (see BIS 1999) contains for the first time requirements on the quantitative treatment of operational risk in the form of a capital charge for "other risks, principally operational risk". The aim was to offset capital reductions on account of increased risk sensitivity when measuring the credit risk charge with an explicit capital requirement for operational risk, where previously there has been an implicit buffer for "other risks". The EU Commission followed this development in parallel with a consultation paper (see EC 1999).

During the consultation process between banking supervisors and legislators on the one hand and banks and their associations on the other, the capital requirement on other risks (see BIS 2001a) was explicitly limited to operational risk as being the most important and best measurable component of "other risks". A corresponding

Figure 4 The structure of Basel

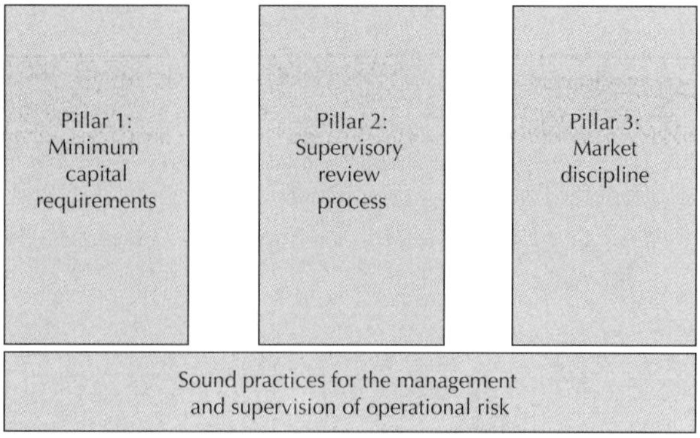

draft of the EU directive was also published (see EC 2001). Other components of "other risks" – eg, the risk of interest-rate changes in the banking book – are accordingly dealt with in the new Basel Capital Accord within the framework of Pillar 2 (Supervisory Review Process, ie, no capital requirement under the minimum capital requirement of Pillar 1).

Operational risk was initially defined as "the risk of direct or indirect loss resulting from inadequate or failed internal processes, people and systems, or external events" (see BIS 2001). Thus, a positive definition (in contrast with the negative definition "everything except market and credit risk") was suggested for the first time in the supervisory discussion, not least as a result of urging by the banks involved in the consultation process. The explicit distinction between direct and indirect losses was dropped in the Operational Risk Working Paper (see BIS 2001b). Since then, the discussion focuses on "the risk of loss resulting from inadequate or failed internal processes, people and systems or from external events". Legal risk is explicitly included in this definition, whereas strategic and reputational risks are excluded. However, detailed consideration shows that an exact demarcation between operational risk and the more established risk types – market and credit risk – is still needed. Examples such as the increase of a default amount due to inadequate management of the collateral come to mind here (see the next chapter for more on this topic).

Figure 5 Overview of the continuum of approaches

- Basic indicator approach
  - one figure for the whole group
- Standardised approach/alternative standardised approach
  - one figure per standardised business line
- Advanced measurement approach (AMA)
  - one figure per internal business line/event type combination

"Partial use" between basic indicator and standardised approaches and AMA is permissible, but a return to simpler approaches is not

The second Basel consultation paper, like the second Brussels consultation paper, introduces – as for credit risk – a "continuum of approaches" for operational risk management, which can be used when determining the minimum capital requirement. Basically, as sophistication increases, the approaches to calculating capital become more risk-sensitive and also more demanding in respect of qualitative and quantitative requirements for their application. As an incentive to select more advanced approaches, and thus contribute to the individual banks' further development along the continuum, increasing capital relief is promised in return for the use of more sophisticated approaches. In this way, the regulation tries to account for the various stages of development and the differing significance of operational risk in the individual banks. Capital savings through more sophisticated models are, however, restricted by a floor covering overall regulatory capital based on all types of risk. In the first year of the implementation of the advanced measurement approach (AMA) in 2008, the capital requirement under Basel II (sum of market and credit risks plus operational risk) is not permitted to fall under the level of 90% of the corresponding results of the calculation under Basel I (sum of market and credit risks); in the following year a capital floor of 80% will apply; and no decision has been made yet with regard to subsequent years.

In the September 2001 operational risk working paper (see BIS 2001b), the regulatory view on sophisticated approaches was significantly altered. Since then it has been possible to recognise banks' own models (AMAs) based on a catalogue of criteria, instead of using a previously prescribed formula (internal measurement approach, or IMA).

Figure 6 The phases of the Basel consultation process

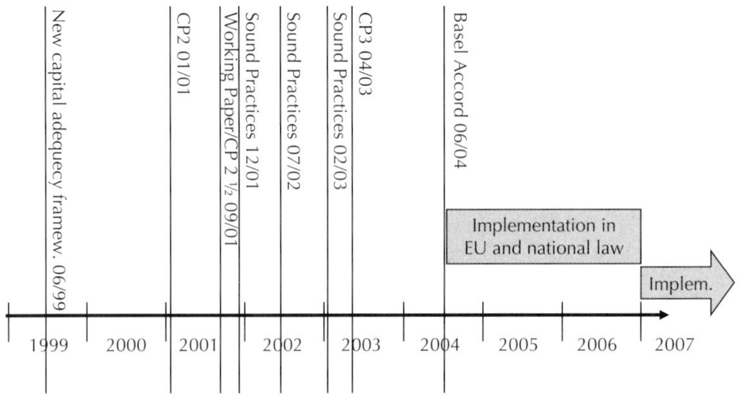

The third Basel consultation paper in April 2003 (see BIS 2003b) contains a more concrete description of the qualifying criteria for the standardised approach and AMAs, including rules covering partial use and recognition of insurance. The third consultation paper on the draft Brussels Capital Requirements Directive (CRD) in July 2003 (see EC 2003) leans heavily on these Basel suggestions.

The Basel Accord (see BIS 2004) was concluded June 2004. The EU Commission's draft Directive was published in July 2004 (see EC 2004) and finalised in June 2006 (see EC 2006). The extent of the alterations to the respective third consultation paper was minor with respect to operational risk and essentially confines itself to clarifications on partial use, Group AMA aspects and home–host regulations, and also to changes to the basic indicator and standardised approaches.

The biggest change lies in the postponement of the initial use of AMA models by one year. Furthermore, the banks are now expected to complete a two-year test period before using the model.

Approaches to calculating the capital requirement

Basic indicator approach

The basic indicator approach is the simplest approach in the continuum of available approaches. It generally can be used by all banks except those that operate internationally or have significant operational risk. The capital charge K is calculated as α times the institute's gross income.

$$K = \frac{1}{n}\sum_{j=1}^{n} \alpha \cdot GrossIncome_j,$$
$$n = Number\ of\ positive\ Gross\ Income\ figures$$

Gross income is defined thereby as the three-year average of the sum of interest income and non-interest income (ie, commission income, trading result, investment result plus other ordinary operating income). Only years with genuinely positive gross income are included in computing the average. The factor α was determined by the supervisors to be uniformly 15% for all banks and businesses, very much driven by the desired average level of capital to be held against operational risk in the banking system.

Standardised approach

The standardised approach follows logic very similar to that of the basic indicator approach. However, it divides a bank into standardised business lines to allow the application of differing factors per business line. This is in order to increase risk sensitivity by acknowledging differing risk profiles in the various business lines. It is seen as the entry-level approach appropriate for internationally active banks and also for banks with significant operational risk.

The capital charge K_{BL_i} per business line BL_i predetermined by the supervisory body (see Table 1) is

$$K = \frac{1}{3}\sum_{j=1}^{3} max\left(\sum_{i=1}^{8} K_{BL_{ij}}, 0\right)$$
$$K_{BL_{ij}} = \beta_{BL_i} \cdot GrossIncome_{BL_{ij}}$$

calculated as the product of a business line's gross income and a predetermined factor β_{BL_i}, the total capital charge being the sum of the individual charges.

A more far-reaching recognition of diversification effects across business lines, which could further reduce capital needs, is not granted. Beta factors of 12%, 15% and 18% were determined for the different regulatory defined business lines.

Table 1 Business lines and their beta factors

Corporate finance (β_1)	18%
Trading and sales (β_2)	18%
Retail banking (β_3)	12%
Commercial banking (β_4)	15%
Payment and settlement (β_5)	18%
Agency services (β_6)	15%
Asset management (β_7)	12%
Retail brokerage (β_8)	12%

The alternative standardised approach (ASA) was developed as a variant of the standardised approach. Here, as opposed to the standardised approach, the indicator used for the retail and commercial banking lines is the credit volume multiplied by 0.035.

Use of the ASA is dependent on explicit recognition by the supervisor, for which it must in particular be proved that the standardised approach would lead to double counting in capital requirements for credit risk and operational risk. Being subject to a national regulator's approval, it is especially aimed at developing markets, where the danger of double counting is considered prevalent.

Advanced measurement approaches

While the basic indicator and standardised approach provide only very limited risk sensitivity due to the footing on gross income, the third level of the continuum of approaches is intended to meet the Basel New Accord's claim to provide risk-adequate minimum capital to a much larger extent. The AMAs correspond considerably to internal models in the area of market risk. During the consultation process it became clear very quickly to all involved parties that there is no one-size-fits-all model for operational risk. Its first victim became the internal measurement approach (IMA), which was modelled very much after credit risk's internal ratings-based approach. Consequently, the discussion was opened up for the development of various institution-specific measurement approaches, contained by a prescribed catalogue of qualitative and quantitative requirements.

Unlike the standardised approach, modelling and determination of capital may take place on the basis of an actual internal business structure, thus ignoring the regulator-determined standardised business lines. Furthermore, operational risk will have to be subdivided according to risk categories (which may also be defined internally) such as external criminality, processing errors.

The capital requirement basically relates to the sum of the expected and unexpected losses (in the statistical sense). As this posed a treatment different from all other risk types, where only the unexpected portion is used for calculation of the capital requirements, there has been much criticism of this. Consequently, Basel II allows non-recognition of expected losses to the extent that a bank can show that these losses have been taken into account within budgeting and/or the calculation of standard risk costs. Then the appropriate amounts may be deducted from the capital requirement.

Regardless of the theoretically unlimited ways of calculating risk capital for operational risk, three main types of approach (in the sense of a straw man) can be identified. Today's discussion centres on the loss-distribution approach (LDA), the scenario-based approach, and the risk-drivers-and-controls approach (see "Bottom-up quantification models" in Chapter 5), but this is not meant to be an exhaustive list.

Table 2 Basel event types (see BIS 2004)

Event category, 1st level	Event category, 2nd level
Internal fraud	Unauthorised activity Theft and fraud
External fraud	Theft and fraud Systems security
Employment practice and workplace safety	Employee relations Safe environment Diversity and discrimination
Clients, products and business practices	Suitability, disclosure and fiduciary Improper business or market practices product flaws Selection, sponsorship and exposure advisory activities
Damage to physical assets	Disasters and other events
Business disruption and system failures	systems
Execution, delivery and process management	Transaction capture, execution & maintenance monitoring and reporting Customer intake and documentation Customer/Client account management Trade counterparties Vendors and suppliers

Qualification criteria for the different approaches

The use of the different approaches of the continuum is tied to compliance with predetermined qualification criteria. These are closely connected to the qualitative criteria of Basel II's Pillar 2 (Supervisory Review Process).

All banks – and thus also users of the basic indicator approach – are expected to fulfil the minimum standards defined in the "Sound Practices for the Management and Supervision of Operational Risk" paper (see BIS 2003a).

Banks must fulfil requirements going beyond this paper to be admitted to the standardised approach. These include both more qualitative requirements (effective risk management and control) and more quantitative criteria (assessment and validation). The qualitative requirements are essentially aimed at the implementation of a clearly defined and comprehensive process for the management of operational risk – ie, involving the board in the evaluation of risks and risk reporting, the implementation of a centralised risk management function and clarification on the role of internal audit.

The quantitative criteria include both data and the methodological requirements necessary for calculating the capital requirement (ie, gross income and its mapping to the supervisory business lines) as well as more far-reaching steps (beginnings of systematic, bank-wide collection of loss data). Here the Basel and the Brussels papers display the largest differences with regard to the qualification criteria. While the CRD is limited to a relatively generalised and short requirements catalogue, Basel II contains an extensive catalogue of criteria for admitting internationally active banks to the standardised approach, which differs only marginally from that for the AMA. The main differences lie in the substitution of the concept of "risk measurement" by "risk assessment" for the standardised approach and also omission of the requirements for a risk measurement system.

The fulfilment of all defined criteria for the standardised approach, together with a number of more far-reaching requirements, is necessary for admittance to the AMAs. The qualitative requirements essentially call for the complete integration of the calculated risk measures into the operational and strategic management of the bank (in particular by the allocation of economic capital). The quantitative criteria include an IT-supported, reliable and comprehensive intra-group collection of loss data with several years' historical data as well as adequate methods of supplementing such internal data with adjusted, quality-assured external data and scenario analysis. Additionally, a bank's respective business environment and control factors need to be taken into account. Furthermore, validation of results obtained by means of stress tests is required. All process steps (establishing the framework for operational risk, the data-collection process, implementation of measurement and validation of the results) are subject to supervisory oversight.

Each AMA model must contain several main components. Internal loss data must be available with a history of at least five years (for a transitional period on initial application of AMA models three years is sufficient). External loss data, scenario analysis and also qualitative components (business and control environment, eg, ratings from risk assessment or key risk indicators) must also be used. Taking insurance into account in order to reduce capital requirements is possible under predefined conditions.

The aim is the calculation of a value-at-risk (VaR) comparable with a confidence level of 99.9% over a one-year horizon. For this, traditionally rare major or catastrophic events have to be explicitly covered, one possibility for this being the use of scenario analysis techniques. The modelling results must subsequently be validated.

Table 3 Major qualitative requirements for advanced measurement approaches

Independent unit for developing and determining methods to support the process of managing operational risk
Integration of results into daily risk management, in particular into the internal allocation of capital to business lines
System of reporting to the board of management and senior management concerning actual and potential operational risks
Documentation of the risk management system
Audit of the entire process of managing operational risk by internal or external auditors
Validation of measurement model by external auditors or banking supervisor (data flows and processes)

Table 4 Major quantitative requirements for advanced measurement approaches

Solidity comparable to credit risk (99.9% confidence interval with one-year holding period)
Coverage of Basel definition of operational risk and event categories
Calculation of capital requirement as sum of expected and unexpected losses, insofar as expected losses have not been taken into account elsewhere
Adequate degree of detail or granularity for documenting the main drivers of operational risk
Basically: addition of individual results; however, recognition of internally established correlations possible
Use of internal data, relevant external data, scenario analysis and factors reflecting the business environment and internal control systems.

Very often, banks transfer risks by buying insurance policies, eg, against fire damage or criminal activities by third parties. In addition to these traditional insurance policies, insurance products are currently being developed that do better justice to the specific needs of operational risk (eg, by covering a broader range of individual risks, increased cover and modified payment terms).

Assuming appropriate contractual design, this approach can lead to a reduction in the frequency and/or impact of losses from operational risk. A corresponding reduction in the capital requirement is therefore desirable and possible on evidence of the effectiveness of the transfer of risk. In addition to the actual contractual terms, any reduction will depend also on the financial strength of the contracting party and the speed of any payment that may be required. In particular, there is a requirement that insurance policies can be recognised only where the insurer has at least a BBB rating; if it belongs to the bank group, reinsurance is required. The extent of the insurance coverage with respect to operational risk must be precisely described. The original contract period must be at least one year and the notice period 90 days; for shorter periods an adequate reduction must be made in the allowance. A reduction in regulatory capital up to 20% is generally possible.

Further components of the regulations and timeframe

An important point in the application of Basel II and the CRD is the treatment of foreign subsidiaries. Cooperation between the banking supervisory body of the host country and that of the domicile of the parent company is necessary here (home–host supervision). If all requirements are met, the parent is permitted, with the assent of all supervisory bodies involved, to determine the capital requirement of a non-significant subsidiary according to a group AMA, which is allowed to take diversification effect across the bank group into account. In contrast to Basel II, the CRD does not differentiate betweeen significant and non-significant subsidiaries; under this regime, the permission of the home supervisor is sufficient.

To facilitate the development of banks towards full AMA application, they are allowed to use an AMA for parts of their business only, and the basic indicator or standardised approach for the rest (so-called partial use), provided the entire bank is covered with the sum of both approaches. Apart from narrowly defined exceptions, the permanent application of partial use is not permitted by Basel II, while CRD is more open in this respect.

The second pillar of the new Basel and Brussels capital accords, the supervisory review process, complements the first pillar (minimum capital requirement) with respect to all types of risk. It generally furthers the development of banks with respect to centralised risk management and aims in particular for an internal capital allocation appropriate to the actual risks. Within the framework of this review process, compliance with minimum requirements for admittance to the more sophisticated approaches and also with "Sound Practices" will be assessed.

The supervisory review for operational risk includes all aspects of the selected approach for calculating the capital requirement in accordance with Pillar 1. In addition, the overall state of operational risk management and control, including internal audit and all risk-mitigation measures, will be taken into account. Non-compliance with requirements or an insufficient level of implementation will lead to measures being taken by the supervisory body.

Disclosure of the required minimum capital and of the methods applied to determine this capital are required under Pillar 3. The extent of the disclosure depends both on the size and importance of the company concerned and on the approach chosen.

Asset-management companies will probably receive similar regulations via a corresponding EU directive (UCITS III, being replaced by the Markets in Financial Instruments Directive (MiFID)); in the insurance sector a very similar directive is currently being addressed in the "Solvency II" discussion.

3

Operational Risk in the Context of All Risk Types

Appropriate organisational structures and risk management processes for market and credit risks have been established within most banks for several years. In most institutions, a similar approach to operational risk management is still in a very early phase of implementation.

As a comparison between these risks shows, the portfolio elements (or areas in scope) that are supposed to be subject to operational risk management are more abstract or at least more heterogeneous than they are for market or credit risk. Equally complicating is the fact that the exposure to operational risk is limited only by the liquidation value of the enterprise.

Figure 7 Structural differences between risk types

	Level of observation	Risk categories	Portfolio elements	Exposure	Max. number of losses
Market risk	Trading desk/ portfolio	Interest/FX/ rate risk	Securities	Market value (except short selling/derivatives)	Number of securities
Credit risk	Loan portfolio	Segments	Loans	Volume of credit	Number of loans
Op risk	Business area	Event categories	Processes	Unlimited	Unlimited

Figure 8 Operational risk as the cause of losses

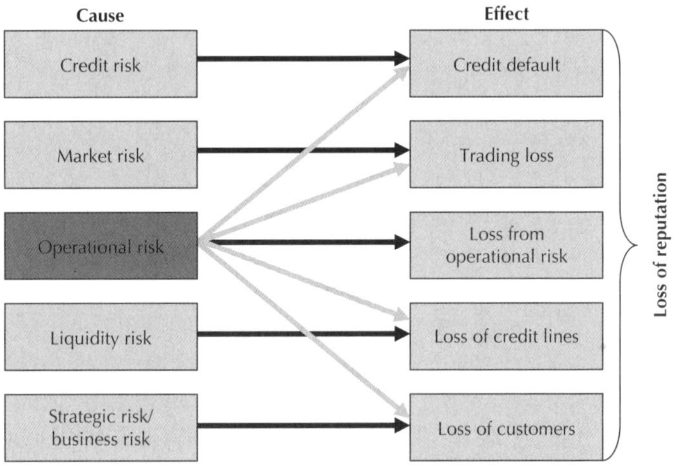

Some banks have defined further risk types, such as liquidity risk, business risk, strategic risk and reputational risk, and include these in the scope of their risk management. In view of the number of potential overlaps, it becomes clear, however, that a consistent demarcation between the various risk types is needed.

Closer analysis makes it particularly apparent that many losses find expression in an event typical of one type of risk, but that they stem from operational risk or are to a considerable extent caused by it.

Overlaps to credit risk

A large number of losses in the credit area cannot be considered as genuine credit risk, as they result from events in the area of operational risk. Examples are credit default cases in which the process leading to the lending decision was not correctly performed and a false rating was assigned to the engagement. Credit fraud can also lead to the erroneous granting of a loan. Inadequate collateral management can result in a loss on a credit engagement bigger than expected. These examples show that in many cases a complete assignment of losses to exactly one type of risk is neither correct nor useful. Assuming that the credit default in the latter example is to be assigned to credit risk, at least the portion resulting from inadequate collateral management should be assigned to operational risk.

Regardless of these conceptual issues, these credit defaults are currently fully assigned to credit risk for purposes of calculating supervisory capital.

Overlaps to market risk

In the market risk space, too, examples of losses can be found that have until now been assigned to market risk only, but conceptually belong to operational risk in full or parts. One example could be a loss from trading in financial securities for which the dealer had no authorisation (either because the specific product is not in his product list or because the limit for this product was exceeded with the transaction). Another case that clearly falls into the area of operational risk is the one of mistrades due to errors during data entry. Slow-reacting computers can provoke false entries when a key is repeatedly pressed. Realisation of the position, given a corresponding decline in price between buying and selling times, can lead to a loss currently reflected in the trader's P&L to its full extent. Assigned based on the root cause, it would belong in the operational risk bucket, as the cause of the loss was a procedural one. Had no mistakes been made, it would not have occurred.

A process for segregating risk types

The segregation of risk types needs to be reflected in all steps of the relevant risk management process described in the following chapters – ie, identification, assessment, reporting, management and supervision. In particular, the opportunities for risk mitigation are often bigger in the case of operational risk than in the case of market and credit risks, owing to the endogenous nature of this type of risk (causation mainly within the bank instead of by external market movements), so that segregation can have direct advantages. On the other hand, complex and thus not generally assessable consequences for regulatory capital as well as potentially negative tax effects (eg, the release of provisions for impending credit defaults) can follow from a reassignment of risk events.

The segregation procedure must be precisely defined to avoid distortions in the consideration of the risks based thereon. Thus, it is necessary to account for the fact that all risk types need a minimum data history for quantification purposes; this implies a certain period of parallel application until a sufficient data history under the new rules is available, allowing for a recalibration of all risk types. A retroactive reassignment – as initially discussed in the consultation process – appears impracticable, at least in the case of larger institutions. Assignment to one or more risk types – also in full or proportionately – should basically be driven on the basis of causes. However, a necessary detailed analysis of the causes can, from a cost/benefit perspective, be justified only for material losses; smaller losses (eg, in the area of consumer credit) can probably be assigned on the basis of statistical procedures (based on a ratio of credit defaults induced by operational risk based on a sample and application to the entire portfolio).

Aggregation of risk types

For management purposes within a risk-reward model (such as risk-adjusted return on capital – RAROC), all individually measured risks must be combined to a total figure. Since VaR methods are typically used to measure individual risks, a simple summation of the individual values would lead to an overstatement of the total risk. This is due to the fact that VaR measurements are based on high quantiles and thus on rare events (nearly of a worst-case nature). A simple summation of high quantiles implies the simultaneous occurrence of several worst-case scenarios and thus a perfect correlation of the risk types with each other. Although a certain correlation of events belonging to different risk types cannot be excluded, the assumption of a perfect correlation is unrealistic and so leads to very conservative results.

There is no simple solution for avoiding this situation, as the ongoing search for integration techniques for market and credit risks clearly shows. The ideal method would be a joint modelling of the factors influencing all risk types. This would enable correlations between risk types to be taken into account already at the factor level. One pragmatic approach, which however carries the danger of significant distortions, lies in the "root of the sum of the squares" method. This formula – modified by correlations and/or covariances if necessary – is valid only if the VaR is a multiple of the standard deviation. This applies only to normal distributions with an expected value of zero. Since credit and operational risk tend to be badly characterised by normal distributions, other, skewed and "fat-tailed" distributions are generally used, to which this connection does not apply. Moreover, both credit and operational risk possess expected values that differ distinctly from zero. More modern methods are based on the actuarial theory of copulas, with which dependency structures can be modelled efficiently.

In addition to the segregation of and integration with market and credit risks, other risk types, such as business, strategic and reputational risks, raise segregation issues as well. Reputational risk in particular is, by definition, mainly the consequence of other risk events. Thus, for example, public knowledge of a longer-term breakdown of a bank's central computer can lead to negative publicity and a corresponding decline in customer loyalty (customers leaving, reduced acquisition of new customers). As the sources of reputational risk lie in the occurrence of risk events belonging to other risk types, it is advisable to handle the risk within the framework of the risk type triggering it.

Figure 9 Reputational risk as a secondary risk

4

Steps in the Process of Managing Operational Risk

In principle, the process of managing operational risk is based on the same steps as those for market and credit risks. Distinctive features of operational risk cause the concrete characteristics of the individual steps of the risk management process to diverge – at times considerably – from the corresponding approach to market and credit risks. The main reasons for this are the fact that they are not limited to and centrally managed in specific organisational units, like market risk in the trading or asset/liability management department; and the fact that they cut across the entire organisation; and the heterogeneity of the components of operational risk.

Figure 10 The process of managing operational risk

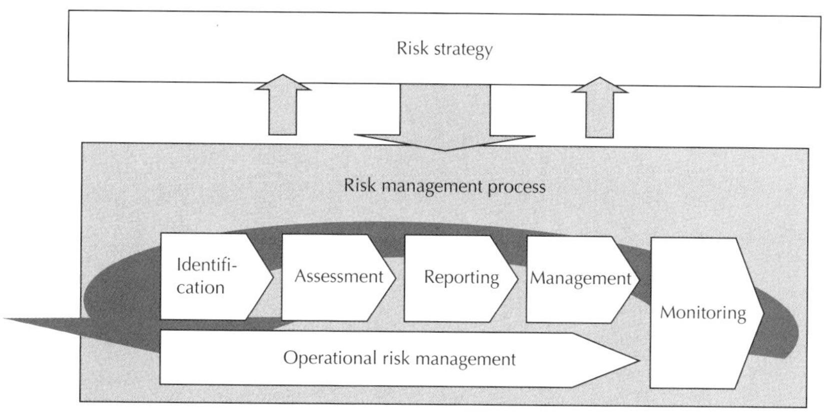

IDENTIFICATION

Identifying operational risk is aimed at the discovery and collection of all information relevant to the management of operational risk. This includes in particular losses arising from but not restricted to operational risk. Further essential objects are the detection of near misses and risk potentials, as well as indirect leading or lagging information on risk such as risk indicators. Depending on the specific type of information, this can or must be obtained in different ways.

Loss data

It was assumed for quite some time that the relevant historical loss data was – although dispersed – to a large extent available in banks' IT systems and could in ideal circumstances be extracted from existing accounting databases, internal audit or quality management departments. It has become apparent that these databases, insofar as they exist at all, are of varying quality, generally do not permit reconciliation with each other, and overall are set up and maintained according to aims serving completely different purposes. Experience shows that none of these databases fulfil the requirements for the identification of losses from operational risk in a comprehensive manner. The necessary scope of data deriving from the definition of operational risk mainly goes beyond the defined scope of an internal audit database; information is recorded in the general ledger according to the criteria of accounting rules and not much else. Quality management databases, on the other hand, document a partial aspect of operational risk, whereby collecting the necessary quantitative information plays only a subordinate role.

Thus, in the medium term, only the implementation of a dedicated database for operational risk based on a clearly defined identification process promises the required level of content. Due to dependence on primarily manual identification and documenting, the necessary completeness can be achieved only by means of intensive training, adequate provision of incentives for reporting, and reconciliation with other data sources. Since most of these elements require a substantial learning process on the part of the staff, concessions regarding quality must be made during the implementation phase. Furthermore, the subjectivity of manual identification and also the reluctance of people, especially when they are involved, to report negative information, can never be completely eliminated. Therefore an absolutely complete recording of losses will not be achievable in this way even in the long term (see Chapter 5: "Internal loss data", p 75). Nevertheless, the aim remains to generate objective data to a large extent without manual influence or disparate media. This will have to happen through improved procedures of data identification and extraction from existing or newly implemented, possibly heterogeneous IT systems.

External data plays a special role in this context. It can stem from three main sources: own research, commercial data suppliers and participation in data consortia. Identification efforts arise only in the case of own research; in both other cases the data will be supplied from outside in a predefined structure. The problems described for internal loss data consequently exist for external loss data as well (see Chapter 5: "External loss data", p 81).

Near misses

The impossibility of directly observing near misses lies in their nature. What has not occurred can hardly be seen. Elements of an enterprise are observable, in particular the existing infrastructure and the processes of producing services. But, as long as there is no malfunction leading to a loss event, there remains only the potential for such an event to occur. However, these elements can, in a clearly defined framework, be subjected to regular or continuous analysis with regard to their risk potentials, depending on the concrete object of observation. To support the operational risk management adequately, what-if analysis and other more elaborate techniques can lead to a more appropriate risk profile than the aggregation of real events can. This approach is used in particular in risk self-assessments and scenario analysis (see Chapter 5: "Risk assessment", p 87).

A special role is played by gains from operational risk such as, advantageous price movements on erroneously purchased securities. These nevertheless represent examples of process errors or mistakes, which could easily have gone the other way. They should therefore be taken into account as events, at least from a qualitative point of view and not be used to offset losses for purposes of operational risk management.

Indicators

Indicators supply only indirect information about operational risk losses; they are therefore considered proxies. Based on an assumed connection between one or more indicators and potential or observed losses, from each indicator change a conclusion is derived concerning the occurrence of such losses.

The fundamental problem with all indicators is the connection between changes in indicator value and changes in the level of operational risk, which can, at least initially, only be assumed in most cases. It cannot always be directly derived, even where it seems plausible at first glance. For example, losses due to errors stemming from employees working beyond their capacity level (due to a shortage of resources, for instance) can relatively easily be forecast. However, experience shows that, with employees working under too little pressure, concentration and focus may deteriorate, which results in more mistakes than expected. Accordingly, indicators and their assumed relationship to risk, need to be thoroughly analysed before they are used to predict or better identify actual events. Risk can also become evident in reduced "performance" just as much as in a supposed "risk indicator".

The determination of indicators is subject to relatively minor subjectivity and arbitrariness, since, once identified, they can be simply determined and verified. However, their disadvantage remains with their initially uncertain relationship to the frequency and impact of risk. This can – if at all – be substantiated empirically only by building up a long-term data series and comparison with loss data.

All three of these essential types of information regarding operational risk display differing characteristics with respect to their usefulness for managing operational risk and the level on which they can be used.

Risk potentials and near misses display a great degree of subjectivity, but in return provide a desired forward-looking orientation, as they are not based on historical observation. Indicators can be objectively determined to a large extent; however, a relationship to a frequency or impact of a risk must first be proven over a longer period of time.

An improvement in the quality of information can indeed be expected through the broadening of the information base, improving identification processes and the increased options for reconciliation among all these sources of information. But the obvious shortcomings will remain in the medium term. Therefore, in the endeavour to obtain the most comprehensive information possible, the existing shortcomings must be taken into account correspondingly in subsequent process steps and their weaknesses mitigated by combining the available sources. From this follows the necessity for an underlying data structure for all sources (see "Definitions and structures" in Chapter 5).

ASSESSMENT

The value of an object or a right – more closely related to financial risk: of a position or a contractual relationship – can be understood as its price. In this respect assessment is thus the same as price determination. It can lead to simple, relative statements such as "high/low" or, more quantitatively, an index that directly reflects a unit of risk (VaR) or similar.

The identification of information to support future management decisions can be seen as the overarching aim of every assessment for management purposes. Directly relating to risk management, this process step is concerned with determining the value or price of a risk taken or considered to be taken. The collection of information of any kind, and of historical data in particular, makes sense in this respect only if conclusions about future developments can be derived from it. Which specific targets are used for management purposes and which methods of valuation are applied can differ considerably according to scope, time frame and information quality.

Application of the concept of determining a value or a price in the area of market or credit risk is relatively simple. Net present values of a market position or a loan can – at least conceptually – be relatively easily determined and turned into price-relevant information (via market or creditworthiness changes), and the risk due to a potential loss of value.

The transfer of this concept to the area of operational risk appears somewhat more difficult, depending on the target chosen. Here, values or prices of risk positions must be determined that result from the design of a process and its embedded control system, the quality of the work of employees or the functionality of IT systems. These are seldom tradable on a market, and thus market prices are available only in exceptional cases and are often subject to short-term changes, making dependence on practical or past values more difficult. Price determination is therefore almost always dependent on subjective estimates, making general acceptance of a value or a price more difficult, and so can lead to varying estimates and consequences.

Nevertheless, for some time now, assessment of operational risk has been undertaken in many areas, without this always being explicitly understood as a process step as such. The main aim is in any event a qualitative or quantitative estimate of the frequency and consequences of the occurrence of individual operational risk events.

Indicators

Even simple "indicators" can give relevant "prices" for short-term steering purposes at the micro level. Assessment then often takes place relatively and implicitly through the definition of threshold values, and the exceeding of or falling below triggering warning signals, and brings measures with it. Results are mainly statements of the form "too high/too low", which, in the area of error ratios or data throughputs, leads to meaningful management information at the selected level of observation.

However, a comparison with barely similar processes or the aggregation of various indicators to one value – eg, across different business lines of the enterprise – is hardly possible. While statements such as "fundamentally too high a cancellation ratio" are possible, the value or price of the risk immanent in the process can barely be determined at a higher level, since a direct connection with a concrete loss exists in only a few cases. While the basic connection between employee fluctuation, work quality and thus, in consequence, earnings is undisputed, it is difficult to make a concrete valuation. A statement about the concrete price of a different fluctuation, and thus a cost–benefit analysis of corresponding staff policy measures of interest for risk management, cannot be supported by indicators.

Equally, it is hardly possible to make a management decision concerning the fundamental alteration of a process, investments in better systems or an increase in staff capacities on the basis of indicators. Their dimension does not permit any price statements that could for instance flow directly into an investment decision.

However, assuming a consensus with regard to the fundamental trend statement of indicators, their great advantage is their comparatively simple and objective determination.

Loss data

Historical loss data can offer improved support for decision making in comparison with indicators by means of simple aggregation without complex modelling. Their property itself reflects a value or price, albeit with the limitation that this is historical.

In any event, a clear definition of the loss components considered in the assessment is essential to the decision making ie, relevant for management purposes. The integration of various loss elements, including indirect losses, the relevance of older data and data from organisational units that are no longer part of the business or from modified processes, must be clarified as to their usefulness for the assessment.

Valuation, in its simplest forms, can take the form of target-performance comparisons, comparison of similar business lines or intertemporal comparisons. The results of such evaluations of operational losses are here primarily of the form that costs that have arisen are considered acceptable, too high or, more seldom, too low. Their advantage lies in the fact that they can be used for future management decisions, since their property already provides the right form.

However, their suitability remains limited for two essential reasons. For one thing, it lies in the very nature of losses incurred from operational risk that they are historical (they relate to the past), and that the recurrence of the events giving rise to them may be uncertain as to probability and magnitude. One example would be a process that was fundamentally changed following the occurrence of such an event. The relevance of such an incurred loss is in this case significantly lower than if no alteration of the underlying conditions were made.

And on the other hand there is frequently uncertainty as to their attribution and/or demarcation, which can lead to incomplete recording or, conversely, to an exaggerated assessment of all relevant aspects. An example for this could be delayed transfers due to a software error. While a clear valuation of the amount of interest loss incurred can be undertaken, the question of the amount and the attribution of the costs of eliminating the error, possibly making use of external IT resources, is considerably more difficult. The occurrence of fortunate circumstances can also reduce a loss, without management abilities having played a role in it.

Scenario analysis, risk assessments and near misses

Assessment forms such as scenario analysis are being increasingly used to perform cost–benefit analyses of insurance programmes or measures for business continuity in case of catastrophes. They attempt – in sometimes complex constellations – to determine the effects of serious events on an enterprise or parts. They are frequently based on specific problems such as failure of the computing centre, unavailability of premises or similarly far-reaching assumptions. Through scenario analysis, an attempt is made to identify all relevant aspects and to evaluate them under various assumptions (best case, worst case, most likely). The evaluation of these risk potentials is highly subjective, since it is either not or only partially based on concrete loss data, but rather on expert estimates. Due to sometimes considerable complexity and a multitude of fundamental assumptions, clear valuation rules are needed to generate consistent and reproducible results.

Estimates of risk potential can also be conducted on a smaller scale. The object of consideration can be a process, a product or a location. Also, their structure does not necessarily prescribe differing scenarios.

Depending on the persons conducting the assessment, it is possible to speak of self-assessments. Other concepts such as cross assessment or combinations of these concepts also exist. Even though no standards for risk assessments exist, there is a tendency to see it as a simplified and highly structured form of scenario analysis. As a guideline, a structure will often be predetermined ie, oriented towards risk categories, processes and organisational units. Frequently, assessment schemes are predefined that attempt to ensure a certain uniformity of the assessment criteria in the event that the assessment is to be conducted independently by various persons in various objects of consideration. The aim here is – in addition to the individual assessment of areas or departments – the comparison of different organisational units and an aggregation of these results.

Near misses play a special role in the assessment of risk. Due to their informational character, they could also be treated as loss data. However, they display a considerable difference – the loss has not been incurred. The evaluation of such events is thus more similar to that of loss potentials or scenario analysis. The determination of a fictitious – since presently not measurable – loss or price for the event stands in the focus of assessment.

Because of the heterogeneous nature of near misses, there are consequently no general valuation rules. In the simplest form the incidents are counted, insofar as they are recorded at all. Their mere identification can be used as an opportunity to change process steps or implement other measures to reduce risk.

A more far-reaching evaluation of near misses corresponds in method to the analysis of risk potentials or, in the case of highly complex processes, to scenario analysis. As in the case of both other assessment methods, clear rules are needed in the assessment process, since otherwise only limited acceptance of the results can be achieved. Thus, in an extreme example, a stuck lift can lead to considerable losses if a business transaction is not concluded on time. But generally assigning this loss value to the time of all stuck lifts would be hard to justify.

The results of all these rather subjective assessment methods will be used primarily for comparison purposes, similar to the simple aggregation of loss data. Thus, the totalling of excesses on insurance claims and premiums paid compared with expected insurance refunds received can supply decision-relevant information concerning the continuation and future structure of insurance programmes. This form of valuation has an advantage over the examination of historical losses, in that assumptions are explicitly made about developments in the future. Thus, management decisions of great consequence – as is the case of strategic decisions – can be based on scenario analysis, since these attempt to evaluate far-reaching and complex situations under dynamic environmental conditions. Their weakness lies in the subjectivity of estimates made by experts, which will mainly be driven by the concrete and historical loss experience of the persons involved. The scenario of an aircraft crashing into a building was certainly always conceivable and sometimes considered in the past, based on corresponding scenarios in the area of nuclear power plant safety. However, the probability and relevance for other buildings would have been considered low before 11th September, 2001. Similarly, the incidence of infectious diseases such as SARS has given the scenario of a building becoming inaccessible a higher probability and relevance. Nevertheless, scenario analysis is not suitable for all areas of operational risk management, because of its time-consuming execution.

Quantification

The calculation of a VaR is considered the most informative assessment method for the purposes of the operational risk management, as is the case in market and credit risks. The VaR states the amount of a loss in currency terms that, in a prescribed period (usually one year), will not be exceeded with a given probability (say 99.9%).

Relative valuation statements can also be made here. The actual aim is an absolute price for the risk taken. The result should be a direct statement about the value or price of the operational risk for the unit considered. On this basis, the interest entitlement within the framework of a bank-wide, risk–reward-oriented management can be ascertained or statements made regarding the level in relation to the sustainability of the risk. Management decisions regarding reducing, retaining or increasing the risk can be made based on this information.

As the determination of a VaR – depending on the structure of the model involved – can be based on some or all of the assessment procedures described earlier, the statements made above concerning their limitations are also relevant here. However, the combination of the various valuation procedures in connection with advanced statistical methods attempts to take advantage of their individual strengths, without impairing the results to too great an extent, by the accompanying weaknesses.

So while, when calculating a VaR, the dimension of the resulting value and the explicit future reference correspond exactly to the target, the complexity of the method is considerably greater than that of other approaches to quantification. Owing to its data requirements, its use is more to be seen in the area of long-term-oriented capital allocation than in the support of management decisions at the micro level of a single process.

REPORTING

Reporting consists of the process steps of collecting, storing and transmitting relevant information within the framework of operational risk management. The quantity of information, the frequency of reporting and the senders and receivers of information must be defined for all components. A largely automated and IT-supported process with role driven access rights may be desirable here, but, in reality with most banks, this is at best available in some business lines or cannot be implemented at justifiable cost. Thus, the relevant information medium, the place of storage and the access rights to sometimes sensitive information must be individually defined and monitored for each information component.

Information collection

The collection of detailed information includes all relevant components such as internal and external loss data, indicators, risk assessment results and the information obtained from scenario analysis. As operational risk can arise in all business lines of an institution, correspondingly extensive reporting is necessary that does not exclude any activity.

Since comprehensive reporting for risk management purposes is as yet not or only partially established at many banks today, the implementation of the apparently simple process can be costly and will be afflicted by friction. This can be caused by the unavailability of information that in some cases must be collected for the first time. Furthermore, it can be handicapped by lacking capacity or because of historically rooted reserve concerning the reporting of sensitive data to other business lines (see Chapter 5: "Internal loss data").

Implementation experience with various banks has shown that, a period of two years for the implementation of an extensive loss data collection process is not unrealistic. The duration depends on the occurrence of the above-mentioned problems, and support from the board of directors and senior management is fundamental here.

Extent and structure of reporting

A clearly defined and implemented process step of identification is a prerequisite for reporting. The exact extent of information is defined on this basis. Thus, the extent in the case of loss data can include, in addition to compulsory information from the bank's point of view, business line-specific elements that are not part of the bank-wide reporting but remain in the business line concerned.

From the point of view of bank-wide reporting, a uniform structure across all business lines and, as far as possible, across the different contents of the information components, is desirable. Only this enables the desired collection of data from the perspective of the entire bank (see "Definitions and structures" in Chapter 5).

Reporting frequency

The reporting frequency depends on the frequency of changes in the underlying data. Thus weekly reporting of loss data could be defined for all events that have occurred. In the area of indicators with very heterogeneous contents, the frequency is dependent to a large extent on the indicator concerned. In particular, in the case of processes with high data volumes, daily monitoring seems desirable; on the other hand many indicators can hardly be obtained more frequently than monthly, and some only annually. Because of the complexity of scenario analysis and VaR calculations, these will – apart from special cases – rarely be carried out and correspondingly reported more frequently than on a semi-annual or annual basis.

Rules for *ad hoc* reporting on the occurrence of special risk events are needed in addition to the regular reporting process described. Threshold events or magnitudes are defined here, information about which is to be given directly to the reporting addressee, usually senior management, at times other than the frequency that otherwise applies.

Differences in frequency are often found between identification and reporting. Except in the case of *ad hoc* reporting, information will first be gathered, aggregated and may be analysed, before being passed on to the receiving function, accompanied by comments if required.

Roles and responsibilities

Only clear definitions of the roles and responsibilities in the reporting process ensure functioning reporting across all hierarchical levels and areas of a bank. In addition to a broad separation according to senders and receivers of information, further differentiation of these roles is necessary. Thus, the recorders of loss data will only in rare cases be identical with those responsible for passing them on to a centralised risk management function.

Within this process, different responsibilities for recording, reporting, quality control and forwarding on of loss data may be defined within one business line, depending on the size of the units concerned and of the enterprise as a whole. Steps for further checks on quality or plausibility, appropriate consolidation and forwarding of information to the various recipients must be established within the central risk-controlling process.

Corresponding responsibilities for those receiving the information must be defined for the report recipients. A regular monthly loss data report to a risk committee will not be handled in the same way as an *ad hoc* report on an exposed embezzlement (see "Definitions and structures" and "Internal loss data" in Chapter 5).

External recipients of information

Reporting to external report recipients, in particular to banking supervisors, auditors and rating agencies, is increasingly gaining in importance. The requirements here are naturally heterogeneous and not always defined in detail. It is clear that external reporting on operational risk will acquire a new quality on implementation of the third pillar of Basel II (disclosure). Whereas the relevant information has up to now frequently been communicated in a rudimentary fashion and often involuntarily in the form of undesirable press reports about the occurrence of loss events, a more important role will evolve for proactive and systematic communication.

One communication channel already in existence in some countries is the risk report within the annual report on the financial statements. Even a simple comparison of available reports from various banks shows that this medium is used in very differing ways. A trend towards standardisation, at least with regard to information content, would be most welcome, since relevant statements concerning operational risk and the state of implementation of its management can barely be made on the current basis. In addition to banking supervisors, it seems fair to say auditors will also apply more exacting criteria as their knowledge of this complex subject grows.

Reporting to rating agencies plays a special and increasingly important role. Only in a few areas is the difference between the information compulsorily required and that which is actually communicated so great. That a bank's rating will in future be assessed in regard to the institution's operational risk may basically be welcomed. Nevertheless, the presently observable approach of some agencies demonstrates a not yet fully developed understanding of the subject matter. An improved structuring of information requirements will contribute here to improved insight into the actual risk profile of a bank.

Whereas the reporting system historically served as regular communication to the banking supervision, external communication will not be able to confine itself in the future. Both regulators and auditors will need get assurance concerning the degree of implementation and the functional scope of the operational risk management within the organisation. Information needs of at least comparable extent can be assumed as far as rating agencies are concerned. Therefore a more structured comprehensive external communication on operational risk management beyond classical reporting will need to be established in future.

Information storage

As already described, automated processes for the collection of data exist today only in very few institutions. The storage of information and its retrieval taking into account the existence of disparate media must be organised accordingly. Ideally, there will be, at least at the level of central risk control, a database that stores all relevant information components centrally, thus enabling the generation of reports for the different purposes and recipients regularly. The technical platform on which this is implemented depends above all on the technical requirements of the bank. Most tasks can basically be carried out with the help of standard PC applications. However, such solutions are often subject to limitations with regard to the recording of distributed data, the degree of automation, the administration of access rights and IT security in general.

Reporting flexibility

Owing to the differences in the requirements of the various internal and external recipients, a certain degree of flexibility in the reporting system is indispensable. Moreover, the information requirements of all parties involved will further increase in step with growing knowledge about the characteristics of the operational risk management. The ability to produce specific reports – of both a regular and *ad hoc* nature – for different recipients will lead to intensified use of information and serve the primary aim of comprehensive risk management.

MANAGEMENT

Operational risk management in the narrower sense makes strategic or day-to-day decisions about dealing with individual risk situations on the basis of identified, assessed and reported risks. The fundamental choices here are between the acceptance of existing risks, their transfer to third parties and the avoidance and mitigation of risks. This bundle of measures is supplemented by emergency and business continuity management concepts that are aimed at limiting loss on the occurrence of significant risks and ensuring the immediate continuance of business operations.

Independently of the level of management, each measure can operate on two components of operational risk: the probability of occurrence and the ensuing effects.

Figure 11 Management measures and their possible effects

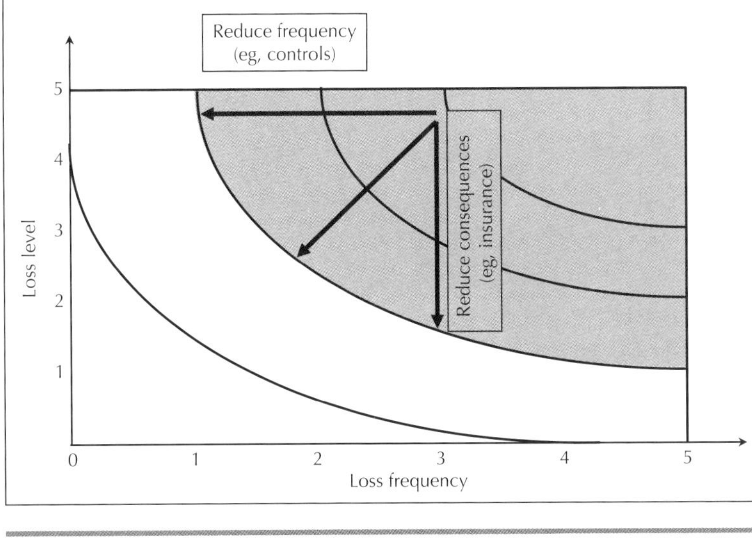

Levels of risk management

Ideally risk is managed on different hierarchical levels. This structure has been implemented in a relatively clear way in the risk market. In credit risk management the situation is more difficult, and, in the case of operational risk, it seems, at first glance, barely applicable.

In market risk management there is, due to the large number of tradable products, a clear classification into risk categories (eg equities, fixed income, foreign exchange), which may be further differentiated within certain trading books if required. For the management of each product there may be, in the extreme case, one manager who controls the resulting risk within the framework of their guidelines (limits). At the next level up, the resulting total risk can be managed in the aggregated form of portfolios according to higher-ranking principles with appropriate instruments. At the peak of such a pyramid is the aggregated market risk position of a bank, the level and structure of which is basically determined by senior management in the form of the market risk strategy.

A comparable hierarchy has been established in the credit area in recent years. Here, too, it is possible to distinguish between the micro level of the individual credit decision and the aggregated portfolio level. Within the portfolios, credit engagements can be summarised by region, industry sector or product. Supported by the development of credit derivatives, these portfolios have now become more easily tradable. Credit risk management now becomes possible at the micro level and also at the portfolio.

Such a hierarchical structure serves the aim of sound risk management. The ability to aggregate ensures that the overall business objective of the bank as a whole can be broken down to the level of individual portfolios, sub-portfolios and to individual transactions. Thus, a uniform and consistent overall approach can ensure conformity with the bank's goals, resulting in a consistent application of the risk management guidelines over all levels. This structure ensures a complete capture of all risk aspects. Clear responsibilities for day-to-day management exist on all levels.

Up to now, in the area of operational risk such a structure with various hierarchy levels in management has rarely been seen. Presumably, the main reason is the absence of a portfolio concept for aggregating a variety of individual risk categories, which operational risk comprises of. Only such a portfolio approach allows management at different levels. The application of the portfolio concept to this type of risk seems possible, at least with its fundamental features, and also meaningful, because of its aim of uniform implementation of a bank-wide risk strategy and clear assignment of management responsibility.

Depending on the aims of operational risk management, two broadly different portfolio structures can be considered: one based on risk categories and one based on organisational units. In fact, both exist and thus determine the management of sub-areas of operational risk. Examples of risk category driven operational risk management are the centralised management of certain areas eg, IT, human resources and legal. However, such a division makes sense only if it ensures the best possible management of the existing operational risk at the various levels in conformity with the business objective. If the risks concerned could be better controlled at some other level, then the principle could not be considered useful. The situation is aggravated in comparison with market or credit risks by the fact that only a few components of operational risk are tradable in aggregated form. Thus, aggregation at a higher level does not necessarily enable better risk management.

Although this is theoretically desirable, in practice the structural principle is seldom consistently applied in the area of operational risk. The examples selected make clear that, in fact, both principles exist side by side and cannot be treated without overlaps.

One business line could, for example, be responsible for managing all components of its operational risk, with the exception of IT,

Figure 12 Area responsibility in managing operational risk

	Risk categories	Internal fraud	External fraud	Employment practices and workplace safety	Clients, products and business services	Damage to physical assets	Business disruption and system failures
Business line							
Commercial banking							

Managed by business line itself
Managed jointly with specialist line
Managed by another line

human resources or legal contracts. It is, however, also evident that the structures are frequently made more complex by the fact that some areas may, within a given framework, be responsible for partial aspects of IT, human resources or the legal department. These structures have usually "just grown" and are thus not uniform over all business lines.

The absence of a binding structural principle basically makes the management of operational risk more difficult than that of other risk. The more complex the actual structures are, the more costly it is to ensure the complete coverage of all risk components as a basis for the clear assignment of management responsibility. A uniform breakdown of the bank's overall goals and limits is equally restricted.

The aim of sound operational risk management is thus a simplification of existing management structures to a point at which a clear management structure emerges that has neither overlaps nor gaps. A desired state has to be developed that permits, on the basis of the bank's overall strategy for operational risk, a breakdown of all goals to the respective management levels. Because of the problems described, this will be impossible to express comfortably in one figure, but will have to provide various dimensions, depending on the concrete object of control. All the more exacting are the demands made on a central unit ie, entrusted with the application and fulfilment of these aims.

Fundamental risk management strategies

In operational risk management, various strategies are defined that could be described as fundamental. A division into four strategies, sometimes presented in the form of a matrix, is common:

- acceptance;
- mitigation;
- avoidance; and
- transfer.

These basic strategies are not specific to operational risk: they can be applied to all areas of risk management. In a matrix presentation they are often shown according to their consequences and the probability of the occurrence of an event.

In the context of day-to-day risk management it is useful to examine the actual effects of measures on each individual risk

Figure 13 Basic strategies for managing operational risk

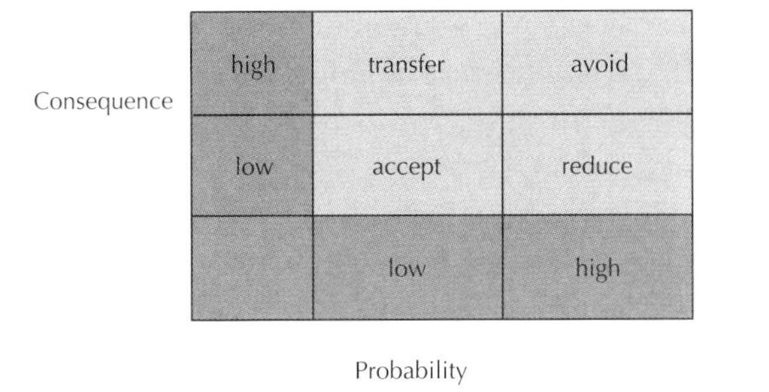

position. This means that an analysis of a measure requires distinguishing between its effect on consequences and its effect on probability.

Furthermore, these strategies are by no means free of overlaps. "Acceptance" and "avoidance" can be interpreted as extreme forms of the same strategy, whereby "reduction" assumes a position between these two extremes. "Transfer" alone displays in some way a solitary position, since here the alternative is offered of exchanging the uncertain occurrence of an event for the certain payment of a (insurance) premium or a fee for an outsourcing service to third parties. However, new risks can arise from this as a result of contracted obligation, or dependence on third parties.

And, lastly, consideration must be given to the question of whether these alternative courses of action actually constitute strategies. In the case of far-reaching measures with significant effects on the risk potential of a financial institution, such as outsourcing IT or the disposal of entire business lines, one can certainly speak of actions of strategic importance, and consequently of a risk management strategy. But this is not always the case, since the same alternatives can also be used on all other decision levels, so it may rather be a matter of operative measures within the framework of the risk management of normal business operations.

The general benefits of these strategies thus lies not in the general statements, which in this form can be directly applied to only a few aspects of risk management, but rather in the simplified portrayal of all basically available alternatives for action. Therefore they outline management's general decision space in all situations more than they provide concrete guidance on how to handle specific situations.

Special risk management strategies

Special strategies within operational risk management are considered to be specific measures or bundles of measures that focus on defined risk components, frequently the majority of the aspects that relate to organisation. They are thus not supplementary to the above-mentioned fundamental alternative courses of action but rather concrete forms of the same.

Notable examples are:

- disaster recovery;
- business continuity management; and
- outsourcing.

Regardless of the way they may be implemented, it is undisputed that the management measures listed here affect primarily the operational risk of a financial institution. However, such measures have up to now almost never been the responsibility of a dedicated operational risk management, but are managed in areas such as IT departments, insurance groups or corporate security.

The reason for this might well be the fact that the discipline of dedicated and consistent operational risk management is relatively new, whereas individual matters highly essential to the maintenance of business operations have been under consideration for some decades.

As described in detail in Chapter 5 (under "Framework"), a uniform structural principle needs not to be implemented for its own sake, but considerably facilitates the complete and consistent operational risk management within the entire organisation. Otherwise there would be no justification. The same applies to such special disciplines of operational risk management. Regardless of their positioning within the organisation, it must be ensured from the point of view of comprehensive and sound management that they be carried out in close consultation with both centralised and decentralised operational risk management. Only incorporating all operational risk valuated management activities into one framework is in the long run able to reduce cost.

This section, therefore, does not include a detailed description of such special disciplines, as this would exceed the bounds of the framework set by the scope of this book. The emphasis has been laid on integration of such specific management measures into a comprehensive overall picture, which is necessary from the point of view of complete operational risk management.

Outsourcing management

Outsourcing and operational risk management have been treated separately from each other for a long time, but are slowly coming together. Initial steps can be seen, for example, in the increasing inclusion of operational risk management considerations in outsourcing transactions. It includes all phases from the initial evaluation via planning to the execution of the transaction. The final phase is the definition, implementation and execution of permanent outsourcing management, which mainly focuses on monitoring the risk management of an external service provider.

However a large number of counter examples of this can still be observed in practice. An identification and evaluation of the operational risk inherent in such a transaction does not always take place within the context of the fundamental outsourcing decision. Frequently, only observations of the supposedly more predictable future costs and revenues are made. The operational risk associated with the transaction and of the transfer, which are in fact characterised by major uncertainty, are not "priced" appropriately. The currently available operational risk management instruments have difficulty in providing quantitative statements here, mainly because of the lack of historical data. The use of risk assessments, however, has shown itself to be a suitable evaluation approach in this environment.

Many outsourcing contracts contain either no or too few indicators that would allow a statement to be made about the quality of the services rendered. If they are defined, they are often calculated by the service provider and thus not easily verifiable by the recipient of the services. Even in cases where this aspect is adequately addressed, there are often no clear rules in the event of non or inadequate performance (service level agreement).

The definition of indicators that can be objectively determined is an essential component of the operational risk management within an outsourcing relationship. It is equally obvious that clear agreements concerning deviations from defined thresholds and limits must exist. In their absence, the recipient of the services can at best only partially manage the operational risk associated with these far-reaching transactions. This is especially unpleasant for the outsourcing customer, as his own customers usually go to him in the case of non or underperformance. The relationship with the outsourcing provider remains an internal one as far as the outside world is concerned.

International banking supervisors have also recognised the relevance of this topic and addressed it in the Basel II document. As the endgame, each receiver of outsourcing service will have to extend his management capabilities to this recurrent part of his value chain.

Disaster recovery and business continuity management

These management measures include activities considered necessary in order to reduce the effects of emergencies to a minimum. They can be very wide-ranging, independently of the object, and include the establishment of rules and guidelines for behaviour in emergencies, evacuation plans, allocation of roles, notification lists, the setting up of emergency workplaces and emergency communications channels, as well as regular tests of all these arrangements.

They are guided by the principle that "disasters are defined by time, not by cause". This statement is of course oversimplified, but it places the necessity of prompt and purposeful action in the event of an emergency in the forefront, if the effects are to be significantly reduced. This presupposes corresponding anticipative planning.

Literature and practice recognise a distinction between the two aspects "disaster recovery" and "business continuity management". While disaster recovery is concerned with the limitation of the immediate effects of a disaster, the purpose of business continuity management is the quickest possible resumption of business operations. As the details of these aspects are not in the forefront of the current consideration but rather their integration in the comprehensive operational risk management, they will not be discussed separately here.

Like all aspects of operational risk management, emergency measures are based on concrete experience by oneself or by third parties. The aspects of emergencies that have not yet occurred can often be analysed only on a theoretical basis, which in turn will have an effect on the measures taken. Nevertheless, a permanent analysis also of external events is of fundamental significance in this area.

Scenario analysis has, as already mentioned, proved itself useful for purposes of evaluating possible consequences. Therefore this technique seems to be a valuable approach in the BCM space, too. To carry it out a group of selected experts capable of analysing all relevant aspects in their totality is needed. Owing to its complexity, this is seldom feasible in a small group.

The analysis thereby pursues two aims: the identification of all potential events and the evaluation of the consequences from the cost–benefit point of view. Of course business continuity in an emergency is of fundamental significance for most business lines of a financial institution, but, on the other hand, backup facilities always involve high costs, since in the worst case they imply holding the entire required infrastructure in readiness in duplicate. This is a significant cost factor, given today's cost of a workplace equipped with up-to-date office technology, and has led to a supply of back-up workplaces shared among different firms or commercially offered by independent providers.

An important aspect of a scenario analysis is the fact that disaster recovery and business continuity management have to come into effect well before the occurrence of a "major" event or disaster. The non-availability of a building can have significant consequences for business operations. Whether this is caused by a local fire, gas alarm or an infectious disease such as SARS is of secondary concern. As a first step, the general risk potential must be identified and evaluated.

In addition to the unavoidable uncertainty with regard to the occurrence and extent of a disaster, the practical relevance and the implementation of the measures defined have a considerable influence on the resulting risk potential. The type and frequency of the emergency drills carried out demonstrate this impressively. Anyone who has ever taken part in a moderate but real evacuation of a larger building – attempting, in a lighted but constricted and increasingly overcrowded stairwell, to recognise floor numbers and luminescent strips and at the same time to devote the necessary attention to colleagues with walking disabilities – and subsequently, in winter temperatures at some assembly point, tried to glean the next steps for a crowd of several thousand from announcements over a not very loud megaphone, will gain a first, vague impression of the actual risk potential and its possible improvement.

Until now, the integration of the interface to risk management has been restricted to evaluation of such events. At most financial institutions, a category of "external events" is defined within the framework of operational risk. Although emergencies can result from a chain of external and internal causes and effects, the most frequent cause will be an external influence. Any comprehensive risk assessment, but also the modelling of operational risk for this highly relevant category, will be based on the results of such scenario analysis. An evaluation of operational risk for a financial institution is thus incomplete if existing emergency planning is not taken into consideration, and will lead to a false assessment of the overall risk profile.

In the future, it will not be the responsibility of centralised operational risk management to play the role of a higher-level emergency management. Neither the necessary know-how, nor the capacity, nor the necessary physical proximity, could be established without duplicating effects. On the contrary, the focus of operational risk management will remain on ensuring the consistent treatment of all operational risk from the more general point of view of the entire institution.

The focusing of specialists on specific areas remains of great significance, as only this can ensure the necessary expert knowledge for managing the complex structures. Equally significant, however, is the clear assignment of such areas of responsibility combined with a consistent evaluation approach for risk potentials. The first ensures an effective risk management, the latter an efficient one.

MONITORING

Independent monitoring assesses the effectiveness and efficiency of the risk management process. This includes analysis of management activities carried out, the identification of gaps in these activities, assessment of their cost efficiency and a comparison between expected and actual results based on defined measures such as actual losses, indicators and risk assessment results.

In practice, such monitoring is a multilevel process, undertaken by various internal and external instances. The following areas are involved in monitoring operational risk, regardless of the actual structure and degree of implementation of an operational risk framework:

- (central) operational risk management;
- internal audit;
- external audit;
- supervisory authorities; and
- market participants.

A detailed description of the internal obligations and responsibilities may be found in Chapter 5 under "Framework", so, for this reason, the process step as such is at the forefront here.

Centralised operational risk management

The role of central operational risk management corresponds with the implementation of the segregation of duties between line management and a centralised independent unit that has been prescribed for market risk by some regulators. The management of credit risks is in the process of taking the same step at present with its segregation into a market ("front office") area, market follow-up ("middle" or "back office") area and – likewise – independent control.

The application of operational risk management is a logical corollary of [or extension to] these initiatives. At the same level as market and credit risk control, frequently also consolidated into one area named "central risk control", an independent and permanent review of all activities of individual risk management takes place that reaches up to board level. The same methods and procedures as are used by management are employed, so as to ensure that managers always move within the framework defined by the board of directors.

Internal audit

The tasks of internal audit are not altered by the establishment of operational risk management, but merely made concrete for this risk area. The essential aim is auditing the effectiveness, efficiency and suitability of the risk management and controlling processes and also compliance with the defined risk management and risk-controlling framework at all levels. Internal audit thus assumes a function in the monitoring process ie, downstream of risk control and includes it.

External auditor(s)

The external auditor's mission is to provide assurance, within the framework of the annual audit of the financial statements, that these statements provide a true and fair view of the net assets, financial position and results of operations as well as cash flows during the business year. In making this assessment, the business operations as well as the economic and legal environment of the enterprise and expectations concerning possible misstatements are to be taken into account.

In making this assessment, the business operations as well as the economic and legal environment of the enterprise and expectations concerning possible misstatements are to be taken into account.

Since the operational risk of a financial institution can have a considerable influence on all these elements, such risks will increasingly shift into the focus of external auditors. It is to be expected that, with the continuing development of measurement methods, auditors will also make use of them. In some countries, the supervisory authorities have furthermore indicated that they wish for a concrete role for auditors within the framework of qualitative supervision. The assessment of the entire framework of the management and control of operational risk will thus become increasingly the subject of external audit procedures.

Banking supervisors

Even before revision of the capital-requirement regulations by Basel II, a financial institution's operational risk and its management have always been the subject of banking supervision. Because of the new and explicit capital requirement for this type of risk, but in particular because of the stronger emphasis on qualitative supervision via Pillar 2 of Basel II, assessment of the quality of operational risk management by the supervisory authorities is clearly gaining in importance.

However, it remains to be seen what implementation of such qualitative supervision will look like in detail. In particular it will be interesting to observe the extent to which use will be made of the possibility of increasing the capital requirement in the event of defects in the risk management system. Clearly, a supervisory authority is emerging that will move beyond present practice in terms of scale and intensity.

This type of supervision will thereby display two forms, a current one within the framework of permanent banking supervision and a special one within the framework of model approval investigations. Both will have significant influence on the basic features of a financial institution's operational risk management. But given existing cultural and historical differences in the supervisory tradition among the countries implementing Basel II, it is fair to assume that different approaches and timelines will be observed within the Basel framework. They may converge over time, but will have very distinct national or regional aspects, as can be seen in the different approaches to Basel in the US and Europe.

Market participants

The role of external market participants as a component of the regulatory framework is relatively new and, in its effects, largely dependent on the implementation of the disclosure requirements defined by Basel II. Basel pursues the aim, through the disclosure of risk-relevant matters, of placing market participants in a better position, or in some cases – depending on previous practice – for the first time in *any* position, to make their relationship to a specific financial institution dependent on its risk situation beyond the credit risk assessment. The decision concerning the establishment, continuation or termination of a business relationship can thus be adjusted to the risk appetite of the business partner and find corresponding expression in the pricing of transactions.

The actual structure of this regulatory role is still largely open, because of the lack of experience in this area hitherto. In addition to general statements on the condition of risk management, the disclosure of major outsourcing relationships in connection with the performance involved or information on the risk profile in certain areas in comparison to a benchmark would be conceivable.

5

The Components of Operational Risk Management

The implementation of a workable risk management process as described in Chapter 4 requires the development of methods and procedures that must be integrated in the bank in terms of organisation and IT. Even if these methods and procedures vary sometimes quite widely in their conception and implementation from bank to bank, all known approaches can be presented in the structure described in Figure 14.

FRAMEWORK

The framework or structural and procedural organisation includes all organisational components relevant to operational risk

Figure 14 The components of operational risk management

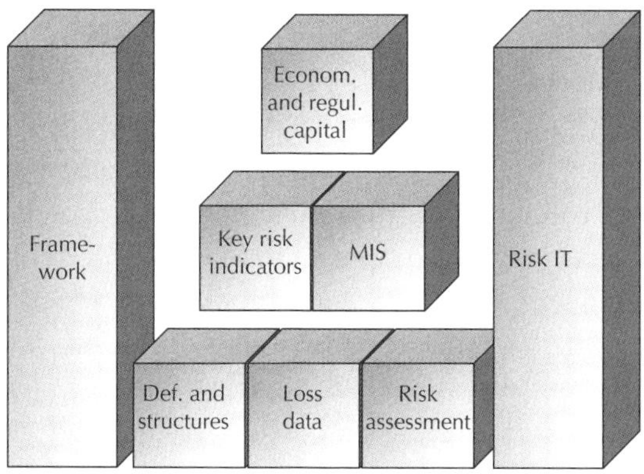

management. This includes the roles and responsibilities at all levels of the organisation, panels and/or committees, the corresponding differentiation from other functions and the compulsory reporting and escalation channels. The framework includes, in analogy to other types of risk, risk management in the narrower sense, risk control dependent thereon and the internal audit tasks specific to operational risk. In the following, risk management in the broader sense is to be understood as any action directed towards the management of risks. This includes supervisory elements such as controlling and internal audit. Risk management in the narrower sense means the decision to accept or mitigate risk as distinguished from independent monitoring and internal audit. External auditors and the supervisory authorities assume further functions. As the last-named functions elude design by the individual bank and as they are regulated by statute as to their extent and structure, they do not represent components of the bank's own management.

The essential feature of the framework of operational risk management is that the corresponding management tasks are distributed from the structural-organisation aspect throughout all business lines of a bank, unlike market or credit risk management. Centralisation is possible in only very few cases.

The approach in the case of market risk

While market risk was historically to be found in diverse organisational units, over recent years a clear tendency towards centralisation has become recognisable. Owing to the specialised expertise required and the high costs of the necessary IT support, most banks have formed central trading units, which are responsible for assuming completely all the market risks of the institution, frequently even of a group. They undertake a risk-pooling and clearing function for the entire organisation and appear in the marketplace as the central contracting party. Because of the peculiarities of this risk and the risk management instruments available, centralisation is relatively simple.

Market risk appears in relation to a product; it is identifiable and – with certain restrictions in the case of less liquid markets – easily tradable and thus transferable. Transfer takes place in the first instance to the central trading unit, which, in a second step, decides on passing it on in part or as a whole via the marketplace through hedging. Existing measurement methods permit, with few exceptions, an unambiguous quantification of this risk at the transaction level and the aggregation of dissimilar products at the bank-wide portfolio level.

As the risk is identifiable in its entire range, a clear separation of the risk component from the actual revenue or margin component can be undertaken. Thus, no customer department is subject any longer to the risk of changes in revenue because of market fluctuations. So it is today only in exceptional cases that market risk remains elsewhere than the central risk management unit. The reasons are mainly of a technical nature, when products are mapped with specific systems at certain locations which, because of their degree of development, either cannot be connected to central systems or, if they can, only with considerable effort. This condition is therefore, as a rule, temporary, or alternatively the costs of connection are in a disproportionate relationship to the benefit.

The approach in the case of credit risk

A similar tendency is detectable in the credit area, although the process is at a significantly earlier stage. The organisational separation between the market areas that enter into credit-related transactions and a central area that identifies, assumes and if necessary transfers this credit risk externally is basically possible.

The less developed markets, compared with market risk, still impede transfer; however, standardised products have been tradable for some time now, and the extension to other credit products is increasing. Within the organisation, the identification of the credit risk inherent in a transaction as well as the aggregation across the entire enterprise is becoming increasingly easier, owing to the improvement in measurement methods. The separation of the risk from the margin component and a portfolio embracing all transactions can be standardised with simple methods and is thus possible for the majority of products and transactions containing credit risk.

An organisational condensation is thus possible for the management of both market and credit risks and makes sense from the point of view of control. Existing methods permit an objective identification at the product or transaction level as well as an aggregation into a comprehensive portfolio view. Units whose objectives are not seen to be the assumption of these risks are placed in a position to transfer such risks to central management with greater expertise at an objective and therefore fair price. This provides the organisational basis for the necessity of further risk management in the wider sense, that of a functional separation of management, independent supervision and internal audit.

Situation in the area of operational risk

As all losses through processes, people, systems and certain external events are by definition subsumed under operational risk, an analogous centralisation of activities is possible to only a very limited extent. Moreover, established measurement methods that would make an objective evaluation possible are not available for operational risk at the present time. An aggregation of these risks at the portfolio or entire bank level is thus possible to only a very limited extent and external or market prices hardly exist. Correspondingly, the decision base and the instruments for a transfer to the market are mainly lacking.

Nevertheless, a clear segregation of functions into management, independent monitoring and internal audit is today also possible for operational risk. Admittedly, there are limitations compared with other risk types, because of the present shortcomings in methods. The advantages of a significant gain in information, the introduction of a consistent approach – usually for the first time – and the considerable improvement in corporate governance following functional segregation cause the implementation of this organisational principle to appear economically meaningful already.

Moreover, this position is also held by the supervisory authorities. Even if current regulatory discussion displays considerable latitude and uncertainty in concrete interpretation, the fundamental statement in favour of independent operational risk management is unambiguous. It is thus no longer a question of "whether", because the challenge lies in the "how". This is to a great extent possible, in spite of currently existing shortcomings in methods.

It must thereby be taken into account that every bank provides organisational peculiarities that must be reflected in the structure of its risk management. Risk management is unlikely ever to influence the historically evolved and market-oriented organisational structure of a bank to any considerable extent. On the contrary, it must take this into account.

An institution that is to a large extent managed centrally at the level of business lines will tend to possess an equally centralised risk control, since this maps the risk structure better than a decentralised one, and vice versa. Likewise, existing regional or national peculiarities, structures and possibly statutory regulations must be taken into account.

In many countries, the setting up of management committees dealing with risk management aspects is compulsory, in others voluntary but common practice. In a third group of countries, corresponding structures are emerging within the framework of the current discussion on corporate governance. Additionally, laws such as the Sarbanes–Oxley Act are having considerable effects on those areas of a bank that are assigned to the operational risk management sphere.

These various parameters have a decisive influence on the design of the entire bank's risk management and thus consequently on the management of the different types of risk. They must be taken into account and implemented locally or throughout the entire enterprise as necessary. The implementation of a specific

Figure 15 The three levels of operational risk management

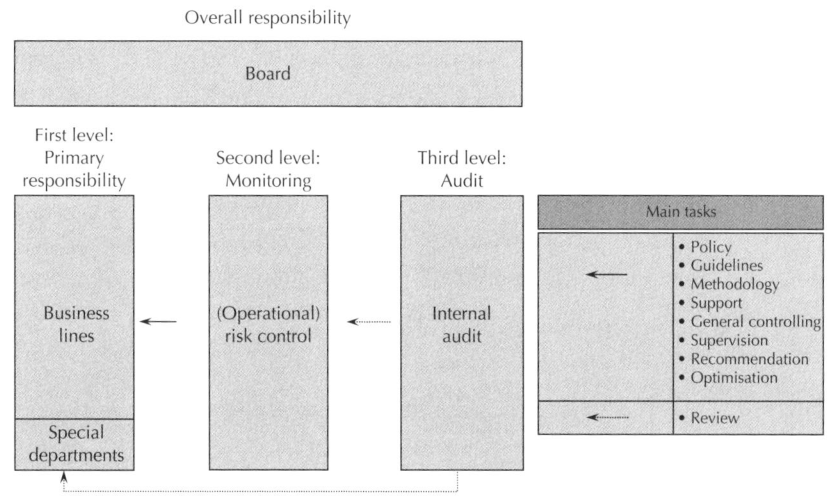

management structure for operational risk is thus in no way dependent thereon. However, it takes place at a conceptually superimposed level and must take the named factors of influence into account as secondary conditions.

The most important elements of a framework are:

- overall responsibility:
  - the board of directors;
  - a committee supporting the board of directors;
- the first level of risk management (management in the narrower sense):
  - management of the individual business lines;
  - management of centralised or decentralised support areas (for instance, IT, legal, human resources);
- the second level of risk management (independent monitoring): risk control; and
- the third level of risk management: internal audit.

While some of these elements are mandatory, such as the board of directors and internal audit, there has, up to now, been no legal or regulatory compulsion to introduce an overall or specific risk committee. Similarly, the responsibility of business line management for individual operational risk is self-evident, but the role of possibly present special units is less so. Against the background of the desired functional separation, a clear definition of the various roles and responsibilities is therefore necessary. In individual cases, assignments that are specific to the bank are necessary, but as a rule the roles are obvious.

Board of directors

As the uppermost governing body of a bank, the board of directors bears overall responsibility for risk management, independent monitoring and internal audit. Moreover, it will possibly be supported in its activities by panels or committees. It is of great importance for operational risk management that the necessary functional separation be implemented up to board level. This will as a rule take place through the establishment of a designated risk director (increasingly also named chief risk officer). Any further specification of their duties with regard to the operational risk management does not appear very meaningful, since this would involve limitations to their overall responsibility.

It is essential that the board receives regular and adequate information about the current status of the bank's operational risk, which places it in a position to address this type of risk to the extent required. Although the regulatory requirements do not address the structure of the bank-wide risk management system in detail, it is obvious that all information relevant to decision making must be suitably prepared and promptly communicated to the board of directors.

Risk committee(s)

An operational risk committee acts as a central coordination and escalation panel for all topics relating to this type of risk.

One risk committee or several covering all or some specific risk types are today in most cases panels that have a supporting function *vis-à-vis* the board, under the chairmanship of the risk director and including expert knowledge from all relevant areas. They therefore derive their mission from him or her and decision-making powers are frequently granted them in the name of the board, but in any event the overall responsibility remains with the uppermost governing body. Their advantage lies in the bundling of specific knowledge, in some cases of a considerably technical nature, which cannot be represented at board level.

Whether an overall risk committee or several specialised ones are established depends on various factors; there are no universally applicable solutions. The complexity of the processes, products and organisational structures is material here, since these essentially determine the risks, as well as the necessary and available expert knowledge.

Thus, the establishment of a specific committee for operational risk, the creation of a subgroup within the framework of an overall risk committee or treatment of the relevant topics by an overall risk committee are all possibilities.

The last of these is more likely to correspond to the management requirements of smaller organisations. Whether an independent committee or a subgroup of a possibly existing one is selected will be marked more by the culture and history of the individual bank than by specific management requirements. At banks in which an established and prominent risk committee always had a wide-ranging focus on all risk types, the creation of a subgroup could be advisable, in order to profit from the advantages of the established panel. Should there already be a committee more specifically oriented towards market or credit risks, there will be a tendency to set up a separate panel for operational risk.

Due to its higher-ranking position, such a committee is not to be assigned to the areas of management, control or internal audit. On the contrary, all these areas should be adequately represented, so that the committee can fulfil its task as the coordination and escalation body with the necessary authority and expert knowledge. The higher positioning also calls for a hierarchically adequate composition.

The clear engagement by the board of directors, the right to information on all relevant aspects of operational risk and the authority to make decisions in emergency cases, should the plenary board not be available, are essential to any organisational form selected.

Business line management

Business line management carries the primary, decentralised responsibility for operational risk management in the relevant area. This is in general undisputed, but in many cases must be made more specific as to how the concept of operational risk and the management tasks and instruments associated with it are to be established and made concrete. Owing to the deep-rooted management structures of, in some cases, many years, there is a danger that all participants agree to the management responsibility of business line management, but possess a divergent understanding of operational risk in general, or of its components, or of the processes and methods to be applied.

The extent of the need for clarification also depends on the organisational structure of the bank. Frequently, support or service areas possess considerable management responsibility, as a rule, for topics with central relevance. Few business lines, for example, are free in their decisions relating to IT; the legal department prescribes firm specifications in all legal matters, in particular in the area of contracts; and human resources implements mainly bank-wide applicable standards for all aspects of employee acquisition and employee welfare. A clear segregation of management responsibility for such special areas is therefore necessary.

Special departments

These frequently centrally organised areas have already been described with regard to their demarcation from business lines. Their existence and the associated responsibility entrusted to them are based on two differing but complementary things. Such an area is either primarily based on its specialisation, which is necessary for the bank's business model but not broadly available, or on the assumption that, for reasons of efficiency, maintaining the availability of this function or this knowledge in all areas would be possible, but not economical or is too dangerous.

In both cases this results in these areas of responsibility for certain clearly defined areas in the operational risk control department. In order to avoid overlapping, but in particular to avoid gaps in the management responsibility concerned, clarification *vis-à-vis* the business lines is necessary, which in individual cases may be subject to considerable efforts.

It must also be clearly defined whether these areas exercise exclusively or mainly management or controlling functions. While the assumption was originally made that areas such as human resources and the legal department are primarily entrusted with monitoring functions, it is increasingly being recognised that central management functions are involved here, which therefore themselves should be subject to independent monitoring.

Risk control

Risk control performs the function of independent supervision. In doing so, it theoretically makes use of the same methods and procedures for measuring operational risk as the management areas. At the present time, in fact, it acts as the driving force behind development and implementation of these elements, in particular in order to guarantee a bank-wide uniformity of approach. The aim is an independent monitoring of compliance with the risk management goals prescribed by the board of directors. These can be varied, depending on the elements implemented. The core components are responsibility for reporting on loss data, the determination of indicators and the performance of risk assessments. The task of risk control is thus primarily the aggregation and analysis of and, if necessary, commenting on the information gathered.

Figure 16 The integration of operational risk into the organisational structure

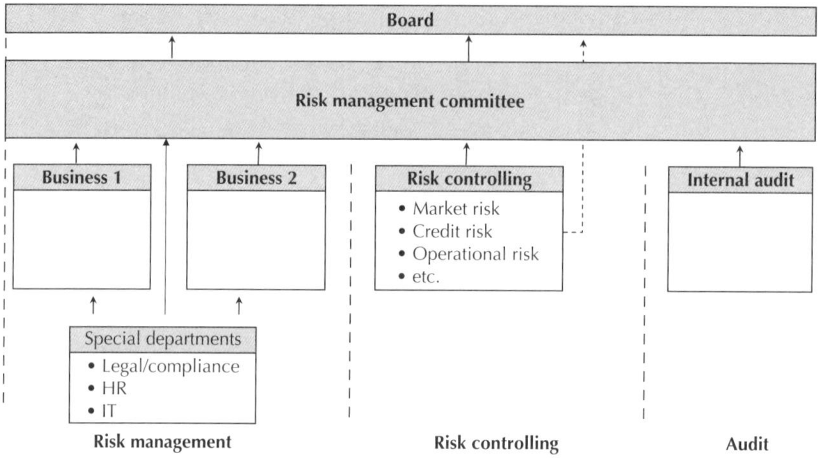

Risk control is also being increasingly involved as a consultant in operational risk questions prior to decision taking. The responsibilities of risk control then include the assessment of operational risk on the introduction of new products and processes, and on the merger or splitting of units, as required.

Internal audit

The task of internal audit is supervision ie, independent of all other areas. Within the framework of operational risk management it must examine the general suitability of all elements implemented and their constant functioning. Due to the fact that it is independent both of management and of monitoring, it creates a third level of risk management in the wider sense. In contrast to operational risk control, it neither develops methods, procedures or processes, nor is responsible for implementation. On the contrary, it examines their suitability and functioning in regular or special audits.

DEFINITIONS AND STRUCTURES

The structuring of all components and process steps of comprehensive operational risk management must be based on a common language and structure. Only this will ensure efficient bank-wide communication using a uniform understanding of terms. Certain concepts that have meanwhile acquired a distinctly different meaning in other areas of the bank, in other industry sectors, in the academic community or in colloquial usage will have to be defined with particular care. A striking example of this is the pair of terms "expected loss" and "unexpected loss", where the colloquial usage (anticipated or surprising loss, respectively) and the meaning in statistics (mean value or deviation from the mean, respectively) differ from each other in a spectacular manner.

The definition of operational risk

Although the Basel definition, "the risk of loss resulting from inadequate or failed internal processes, people and systems or from external events", has by now been accepted by most banks, there are reasons to doubt whether actual interpretation is consistent. This is demonstrated for example, in the fact that the alteration to the definition of operational risk undertaken during the consultation process, consisting of the deletion of the original phrase "direct or indirect [losses]", was welcomed by the majority of banking associations, although the currently valid definition must be regarded as more general, in other words more comprehensive. Moreover, the statement that legal risks are included in this definition needs to be made more concrete. And, finally, a demarcation of operational risk from the other risk types defined by the bank, such as market risk, credit risk, liquidity risk, strategic risk, business risk, reputational risk and so on, is needed (see Chapter 3).

The necessity of a comprehensive definition of all relevant terms thus becomes obvious. These must not only be sufficiently precise, but must also be worded in a way that they can be communicated and understood across all areas of the bank.

Furthermore, agreement on a structure for the collection and evaluation of data valid for all components is necessary. This usually consists of a division of operational risk into risk categories on the one hand and a division of the enterprise into organisational units and/or processes on the other.

Risk categories

Operational risk can be assigned to risk categories in a variety of ways. In practice, hierarchical structures with two to four levels

Figure 17 Structural matrix

	People	Technology	...	Total
Private banking	$Data_{11}$	$Data_{12}$	$Data_{1j}$	$Data_{1\bullet}$
Investment banking	$Data_{21}$	$Data_{22}$	$Data_{2j}$	$Data_{2\bullet}$
...	$Data_{i1}$	$Data_{i2}$	$Data_{ij}$	$Data_{i\bullet}$
Whole bank				$Data_{\bullet\bullet}$

have proved useful, doing justice both to detailed requirements for the recording and evaluation of data and also being able to serve management purposes. All categorising schemes should satisfy a catalogue of requirements.

The most important requirements include the following.

- ❑ Relevance to management: evaluations based on the categories should support management decisions.
- ❑ Intelligibility: high demands on the quality of the data recorded presuppose a common understanding across all areas of the bank.
- ❑ Selectivity: the assignment of risk events to individual categories should be applicable in an objective manner and unambiguous.
- ❑ Coverage: all possible operational risk events should be assignable to a category.
- ❑ Granularity: the granularity at the individual levels of a categorisation hierarchy should be compatible with the existence and/or expectation of data.
- ❑ Balance: different categories at the same level of aggregation should provide similar granularity.

The first possible level of categories is the causes that have led to the occurrence of the risk events (sometimes referred to as risk drivers). These are frequently divided into people, systems, processes

Figure 18 Causes of loss

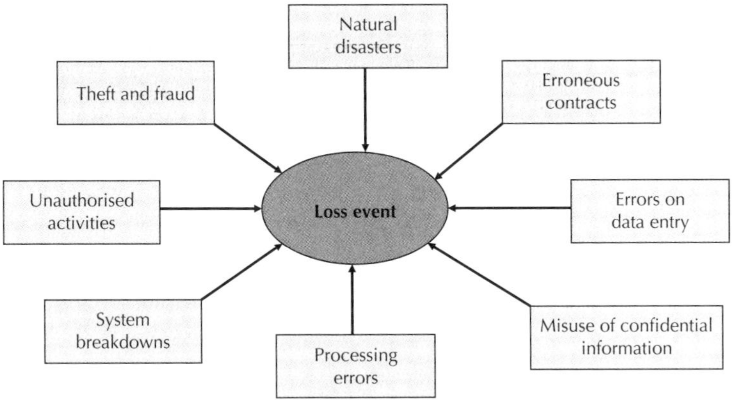

and external events, in reference to the definition of operational risk. One problem when categorising according to causes is the fact that it is often not possible to identify one single cause (multiple causality and/or chains of cause and effect). Frequently a detailed analysis of the causes of significant losses leading to the introduction of measures designed to prevent them is more goal-oriented than the search for a suitable cause category, which can be time-consuming in some cases.

The second level consists of categorising the loss events themselves (eg, false entries, system breakdown and external fraud). This procedure has meanwhile proved to be the most practicable for identification and measurement purposes, since assignment to a single category is easily possible, apart from a few exceptional cases. Furthermore, reports by event class provide a starting point for selected measures. Event categories should be worked out individually for each bank, so that they reflect the risk profile and are usable by all employees. A secondary condition is that they must include all possible risks and be free of overlapping.

Table 5 Example of event categories (Forum for European Discussions on Operational Risk)

Policy	Staff retention
Processing	Employer failure
Product	Unauthorised conduct
Outsourcing	Unlawful internal activities
Legal and documentation	External crime
Technology infrastructure	Vendors and suppliers
Hardware and software	Natural disasters
IT security	Man-made or accidental disasters
Technology in buildings	Corporate culture
	Project management

The event categorisation laid down internally by the bank must be mappable to the Basel event types so as to meet the requirement that loss data can be reported according to the supervisory structure.

The third possible level of a categorisation is the division of the financial consequences of the risk events into accounting classes (effects). If such categories are suitably structured, reconciliation with the corresponding loss accounts of the general ledger and thus a check on the plausibility of the losses recorded is possible (see next chapter). It should be borne in mind here that several losses can result from one event.

Organisational structure

No bank will be prepared to restructure itself for the purposes of managing operational risk, but a practicable bank structure for

Figure 19 Cause/event/effect

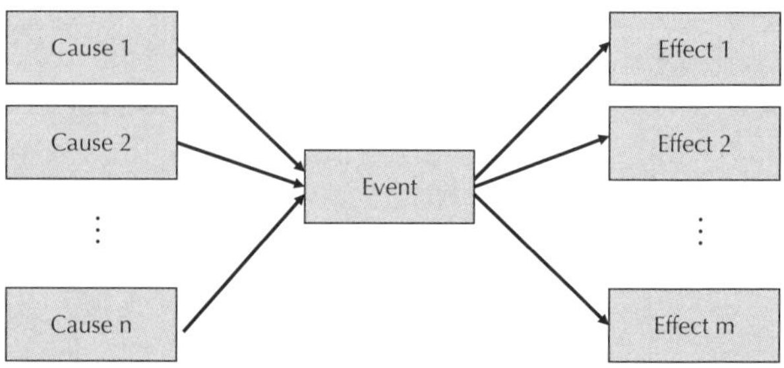

operational risk purposes must be defined. Because of the fact that most operational risk has a negative effect on bank processes, either directly or indirectly, a process view is generally useful. However, this is often thwarted at the practical level by the fact that no one has been given responsibility for the process, or they are insufficiently remunerated based on risk or performance. As the main aim of managing and controlling operational risk should be the triggering of the implementation of measures against it, orientation to organisational structures is more on-target in such cases. Occasionally, approaches may be found in the marketplace that are based on generic process steps, simplifying the comparability of risk profiles between individual business lines. A division into organisational units is usually preferred in practice, for the reasons mentioned. Here, a multilevel structure suggests itself, to do justice to data requirements on the one hand and the possibility of evaluation (eg, for sophisticated quantification models) on the other.

The greatest challenge in mapping the bank's structure consists in adjusting to restructurings, so that a consistent history of loss data, risk assessments and indicators can be built up. In the case of the merging of individual organisational units or processes (merger of the departments B2 and B3 in the example in Figure 20), the re-attribution of historical data should easily be possible; the subdivision of individual old structure components into several

Figure 20 Example of restructuring

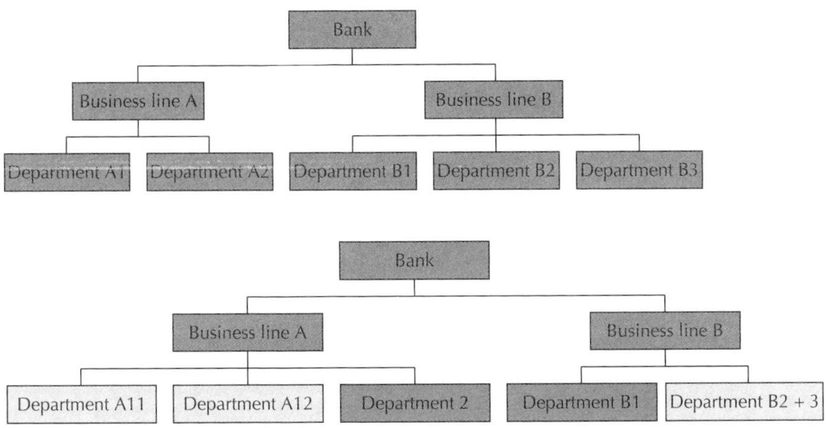

new ones (division of department A1 into the departments A11 and A12 in the example) involves, as a rule, manual assignment.

The bank structure must also be capable of being mapped to the supervisory business lines. This serves the purpose – analogously to risk categorisation – of, on the one hand, reporting loss data in the format required by the supervisory authorities and, on the other, of guaranteeing the ability to ascertain gross income for calculating the standardised approach in the defined business lines for regulatory purposes.

Table 6 Basel business lines

Level 1	Level 2
Corporate finance	Corporate finance Municipal/Government finance Merchant banking Advisory services
Trading and sales	Sales Market making Proprietary positions Treasury
Retail banking	Retail banking Private banking Card services
Commercial banking	Commercial banking
Payment and settlement	External clients
Agency services	Custody Corporate agency Corporate trust
Asset management	Discretionary fund management Non-discretionary fund management
Retail brokerage	Retail brokerage

LOSS DATA

Loss data reflects the historical experience of a financial institution with regard to occurred operational risk events and the financial consequences associated therewith and thus the risk potential realised to date. The collection of internal loss data and the acquisition of external loss data represent a valuable basis for the identification and assessment of operational risk. A loss database makes existing risks transparent, supports the purposeful introduction of risk-reducing measures and forms an important starting point for the quantification of operational risk. Lastly, the collection of loss data is a qualitative requirement of the standardised approach; the supervisory authorities retain the right to inspect the historical loss data.

It should be borne in mind here that operational risk can occur both in the form of easily observable "high-frequency, low-severity" losses and in hard-to-observe "low-frequency, high-severity" losses.

Internal loss data

The majority of operational risk events leading to losses affecting the profit-and-loss account are principally to be found in the financial institution's documentation, in particular in the form of expense booking. Admittedly, it is as a rule very difficult to separate entries relating to operational risk from entries that have no risk origin. This stems above all from the fact that usually no dedicated accounts are used for booking losses and the description frequently does not allow adequate conclusions to be drawn about the origin of the entry. In view of the very large number of expense bookings it is thus often not possible to reconstruct the reasons for the entry on an individual basis. Indeed, in some cases, losses from operational risk are even consciously or unconsciously set off against revenues or posted as reversing entries on revenue accounts. Further sources of information on losses from operational risk are thus internal audit reports, minutes of board meetings, complaints databases and so on.

Loss data collection process

Since the existing sources are, as mentioned, customarily insufficient for building up a reasonably complete loss data history, internal losses by the bank must be collected by means of a special collection process. It must be determined when, and in which part of the bank, what kind of loss event has occurred, with what financial consequences.

It must be ensured in the loss data collection process that all losses that have occurred be reported as promptly as possible. In order to limit the costs of collection in relation to the benefit associated therewith, *de minimis* thresholds for collection are usually

Figure 21 Loss data collection process

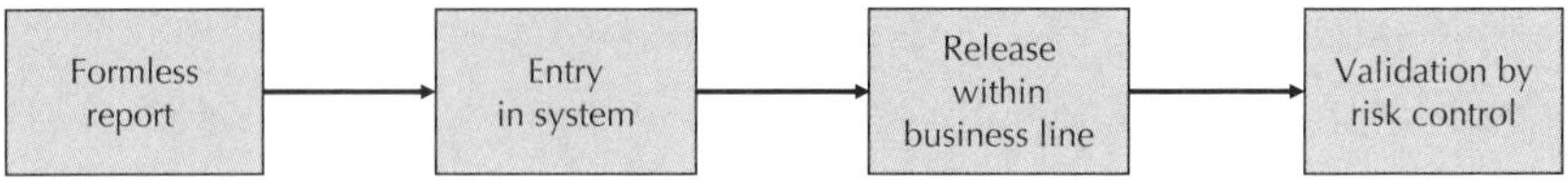

defined. At most banks these are currently in the region of €500 to €10,000.

Which types of loss events to record must first be defined. Direct losses and provisions should be recorded completely, subject to the *de minimis* threshold, while indirect losses, forgone income (opportunity costs) and near misses can, by their nature, hardly be recorded completely and thus only on a voluntary basis.

For the collection of loss data, all employees of the bank must be effectively informed and in particular trained concerning their duties in relation to the discovery and reporting of operational risk losses. Additionally, it makes sense to equip selected employees in each area with a deeper knowledge of operational risk and to establish them as a recorder. The information entered must be checked by a second person and supplemented as necessary by missing information, in accordance with the principle of dual control. Special areas such as the accounting and insurance departments, which supply for example, the book values of damaged or stolen assets and the amount of insurance compensation, play an important role here. A further component of the loss data collection process is a central quality control, which is available in case of queries by the recorder and which checks the consistency and completeness of the information recorded.

Minimum scope of loss data collection

The following data, which is described in greater detail below, must at least be recorded.

- ❑ Organisational unit/process: party responsible or affected.
- ❑ Risk category: classified by event, if necessary additionally by cause and effect.
- ❑ Date: of event, if necessary also dates of discovery, recording, and posting.

- Amount of loss: net amount, gross amount, insurance refund as appropriate.

Organisational units or processes must be classified by structure to enable effective risk management. Basically, the unit must be recorded that, following the responsibility principle, is most likely to be able to avoid similar losses in the future. Of course there will be losses that have arisen outside the sphere of influence of the bank, the occurrence of which cannot be controlled (such as terrorist attacks and natural disasters). In such cases the organisational unit to be recorded must be seen more in the sense of the party affected.

A special case occurs when the unit causing the loss is a cost or service centre. In these cases, the unit is admittedly capable of influencing the future occurrence of similar loss events. However, within the framework of normal, risk-oriented bank management concepts, such units are not supplied with economic capital, since they lack the possibility of paying interest on such capital through the corresponding generation of revenues. An obvious solution in such cases is thus to determine one or more "carriers" to whom the losses are attributed for purposes of determining economic capital. In the case of multi-business line services, a percentage distribution in analogy to the usual cost allocation models can be suitable. As an alternative, allocation could take place via internal service level agreements.

The categorisation of risks is useful for recognising patterns in the occurrence of loss events and thus for the deliberate choice of measures. Moreover, it is needed for efficient use in quantification and also for compliance with reporting requirements by the supervisory authorities.

The recognition of dates is necessary for modelling, but also to permit reconciliation with other sources of data, in particular expense accounts. The date of the event can often not be reconstructed, or the event has continued over a long period of time (eg, in embezzlement cases). In such cases, the date on which the event was recognised or recorded can be used as a substitute. Interesting information can be gained from the time span between occurrence and discovery of an event or between discovery and reporting.

One of the most important pieces of information is of course the monetary consequences of the event. It must be borne in mind thereby that one event can result in several payments affecting the profit-and-loss account. An example of this is the breakdown of a central IT system, which can lead to interest losses by the bank, compensation payments to customers and also expenditure on the renewed start-up of the system. It is fundamentally possible to distinguish between gross losses and net losses. The gross loss is the loss before any kind of repayment or compensation and/or insurance payment. Insofar as cases that go beyond direct losses such as forgone revenue and near misses are to be recorded, corresponding differentiation is required when recording for later evaluation purposes.

In specific cases, a loss can result from a transaction that was up to now recorded as a loss only from market or credit risk (see Chapter 3). These include exchange-rate losses due to unauthorised trading positions or loan defaults where the collateral cannot be realised because of the bank's own internal errors. In such cases, suitable flagging must be undertaken, both in the operational risk loss database and in the corresponding database on the market or credit risk side, not least in order to fulfil supervisory requirements. In the ideal case, such flagging would express the absolute or relative share of the loss ie, also recorded in the loan default history.

Recording additional information

Furthermore, additional information, in particular a description that facilitates reconciliation with other pieces of information, is helpful. Valuable information for a scenario analysis can be derived from those descriptions. Moreover, when a loss occurs, people should start thinking about measures to implement in order to avoid future losses of a similar nature. If mandatory measures are required to rectify the situation that led to the loss, appropriate information is a good idea. The implementation can then later be compared with it.

When determining the amount of information to be recorded, it should be borne in mind that a trade-off exists between quality and quantity of individual information items. In general, the greater the number of individual information items asked for, and thus the time required for an adequate answer, the poorer the quality of the data recorded will be.

Incentives for data collection

A basic precondition for a functioning data collection is an adequate risk culture, which encourages the reporting of risk events.

Unlike market and credit risks, which essentially stem from objective factors lying outside the sphere of influence of the bank and the individual employee (eg, exchange-rate fluctuations or default rates), losses from operational risk are often caused by employees (malicious acts or careless mistakes). There are of course inherent incentives not to report the consequences of one's own incorrect conduct or shortcomings.

Not the least of these are bonus systems that reward for revenues but usually do not sufficiently penalise costs that can arise, eg, from losses from operational risk. There is a complex connection between the number and size of losses incurred and the calculated risk capital. However, a bigger number of losses is intuitively associated with higher risk capital, which leads, other things being equal, to lower risk–reward ratios and thus to a lower bonus. This endangers openness in dealing with losses from operational risk.

To compensate for this effect incentives must be built into the operational risk management system. At the microeconomic level, the expected benefit (ie, the utility function U) of reporting losses (including reprisals that may be associated therewith) must be greater than the expected benefit of refraining from reporting (including the resulting penalties on discovery):

$$\text{U (not reporting)} \leq \text{U (reporting)}$$

Assuming that a penalty presupposes discovery of not reporting (fine given discovery – FGD) and that discovery will take place with a certain probability (probability of discovery – PD) and that reporting is provided with an incentive (incentive for reporting – IR), the above formula can be restated as:

$$\text{U (PD} \times \text{FGD)} \leq \text{U (IR)}$$

The success of an incentive system thus depends on the diligent management of the three determinants PD, FGD and IR.

Controls can be increased by central risk control or by internal audit so as to increase the probability of discovery – PD. This measure is naturally limited by the costs it causes and the possible negative influence on the working conditions.

The level of the penalty – FGD – can be defined by risk control, whereby strong backing from the board of directors is necessary, and the risk culture actually hoped for must not be replaced by a culture of anxiety.

The risk culture is, ultimately, the central factor of success for the IR component. On the one hand it must be ensured that there are no sanctions threatened for reporting a loss; on the other hand a reward for cooperating in the collection of loss data must be promised in addition. Central components of such rewards are a good example and recognition and praise; in the case of key persons in the loss data collection process, the task should moreover be embedded in the appraisal system widespread in many banks.

Building on this, the loss data collection process must ensure, as far as possible, a complete and consistent collection of data. This includes a comprehensive and intuitive guideline that contains a description of the roles and responsibilities of all employees involved, including the escalation channels. Approval procedures graduated according to loss level contribute to high data quality. Additionally, centralised quality control must carry out plausibility and completeness checks, eg, through comparison with internal audit reports, indicators and external information. In addition to

Figure 22 Connection between loss data and quantification

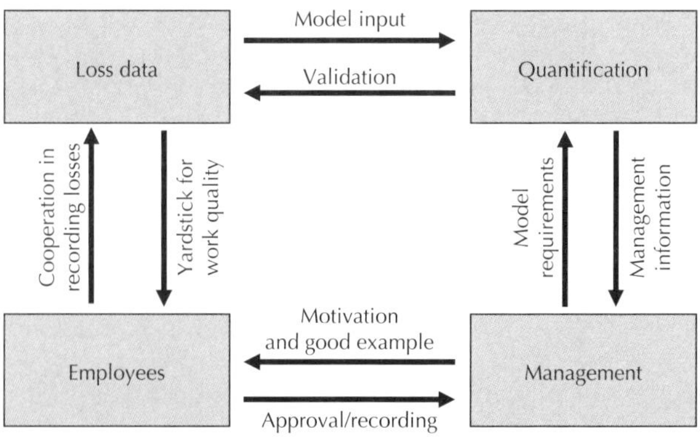

auditing the process of managing operational risk as a whole, internal audit must examine in particular the loss data collection process on a sample basis.

Moreover, a comparison with the balances of the corresponding loss accounts can be carried out. It is advisable in this regard to include accounting information in the loss database (account numbers with amounts and dates of entries) and conversely to transfer reference numbers of entries in the loss database to the booking description. Whether all losses recorded in the loss database were correctly posted and whether conversely an entry is present in the loss database for every booking related to operational risk must be examined. This analysis is made more difficult by the fact that both recording in the loss database and also the bookings are generally made at least a few days and often several weeks after discovery of a corresponding loss event and thus the allocation to the applicable accounting period between account booking and the status in the loss database is not trivial. The successful validation of loss data collection by means of loss accounts on a sample basis requires a longer learning process, since employees must be urged to use the correct expense accounts and to record informative entry descriptions and reference numbers as needed.

In a similar manner, reconciliation between reported losses and insurance compensation received can be carried out.

External loss data

Major losses are typically rare but are important for determining potential risks. Thus, internal loss data collection is by definition only a small sample of the universe of possible losses. For this reason the use of external experience – as the insurance industry does when pricing non-life insurance – suggests itself here.

Basically there are two possible sources of external information.

1. Data sharing

Data sharing initiatives bring together the collected loss data of member institutions in anonymous form. This requires, in addition to defining the scope of loss data, agreement on a common structure (organisational units and risk categorisation), ie, internal data must be translated into this structure. On the other hand the data received from the data-sharing initiative must be adjusted to the internal structure, which necessarily leads to a loss in information. In spite of theoretical advantages of the formation of data pools, up to now only a few initiatives of this type have been founded with a fairly limited number of members each. The main reasons for this are, in particular, concerns for confidentiality and also the not universally recognisable benefits (eg, in view of the lack of uniform data quality, at least in the initial stages).

At present it is an open question whether the emphasis of the data exchange should be on quantitative information (date and size of loss and assignment to organisational units and risk categories) or on qualitative information (description of the event and its causes and background).

While the former can be useful for a classical actuarial approach (credibility theory – see later under "Economic and regulatory capital"), the preparation of scenarios based on the available information is in the foreground in the case of the latter. In the case of purely quantitative data (as practised by the Basel Committee in the various quantitative impact studies and loss data collection exercises), the problem arises of adjusting external data to the circumstances of the institution using them (eg, for size, business model, process and system landscape, corporate culture, legal environment). The methodology sometimes used of scaling the size of losses on the basis of profit, cost or turnover figure appears questionable, in view of the complex interrelationships present in operational risk. In the case of more qualitative orientation of data-sharing initiatives, the problem of anonymity, in other words the confidentiality of the data, becomes more prominent.

The results of the quantitative impact studies and the loss data collection exercises by the Bank for International Settlement (BIS) provide typical loss data collection problems (very uneven distribution of the data).

Two competing data consortia with different approaches are worthy of mention as examples. The Operational Risk Data eXchange (ORX) is an international association, made up of a number of large banks (12 founding members with a similar number of members having joined in the meantime) with high quality standards. On the other hand, the Global Operational Risk Loss Database (GOLD) is an attempt initiated by the British Bankers' Association to bring together a rather large number of banks, the

Figure 23 Distribution of losses according to QIS 2 and 3

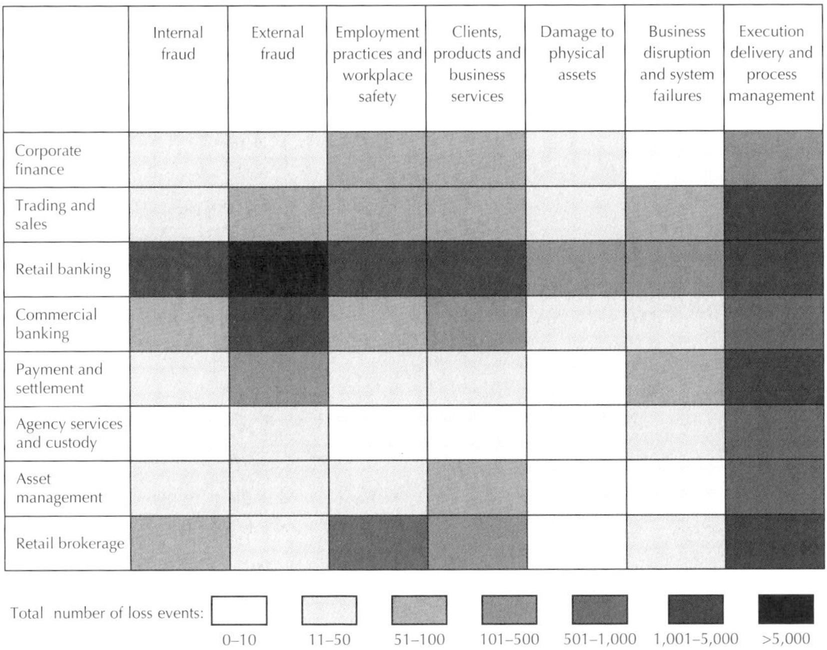

majority of which are British, with consciously low qualitative standards and at low cost. Efforts to form further consortia may be observed eg, in Germany (Verband öffentlicher Banken – VÖB), Luxembourg (Association des Banques et Banquiers de Luxembourg – ABBL) and Italy (Associazione Bancari Italia – ABI). Although the desire to form homogeneous data pools is understandable, there is a danger that none of the efforts will attract a sufficient number of members and that thus the critical mass required to extract statistically valid statements will not be reached.

2. External public data

The second source of data is external public data. This can either be searched for by each institution itself or purchased from commercial suppliers. This involves systematically seeking out publicly known losses in online or print media and recording them in a standardised format. Usually, losses of about €1 million and upwards are recorded in such databases. Naturally, external public losses represent only a small part of the losses that have actually occurred. Not all categories of risk are equally well represented, since some types of loss reach the public more easily than others. Since the information is not first-hand, the loss amounts notified also tend to be unreliable. Furthermore, the fact that the proportion of losses notified varies considerably according to cultural area and legal system is problematic. Against this stands the advantage of having a large number of worst-case events available, which, in the case of a data pool, would require a very large number of members and a long time period, because of the scarcity of occurrence. Additionally, databases with information about insurance settlements for operational risk events are on offer.

Interplay of the various data sources

Because of the peculiarities of operational risk, in the first instance each of the three data sources (internal loss data, data consortia and external public data) has its right to exist. To a certain extent it is possible to draw an analogy with the task of ascertaining, on the basis of empirical information, the possibilities of winning the lottery.

One could start – comparable to internal loss data collection – by questioning a large number of lottery players about their winnings in the last draw. One could indeed obtain a pretty good estimate of the probability of winning (number of wins per number of lottery players). However, the likelihood of deriving a realistic figure for the average winnings or even a big win in the sense of a quantile is remote. This is because – analogously to operational risk – major winnings are seldom, but significantly influence the distribution curve of the amount won and thus its mean and quantiles. It may further be assumed that the collection of data contains errors, since on the one hand individual lottery players will make a pretence of winning for psychological reasons, whereas on the other hand they may possibly keep quiet about big winnings for reasons of anonymity.

The second available source of information is press reports on major winnings. These provide information about best-case events. However, the quality of this information is problematic, since only a small proportion of major wins are reported in the press.

And finally, in analogy to data-sharing initiatives, win quotas and similar information are available from which it can be seen which lottery system the data has been gained from.

Figure 24 Coverage of the various loss data sources

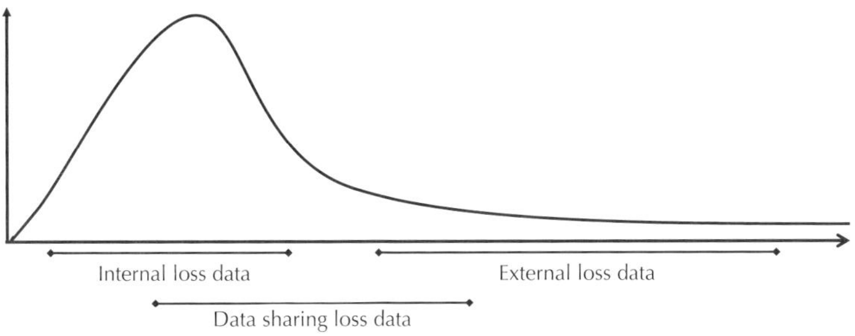

Internal loss data gives in particular an indication of the frequency and the typical size of losses from operational risk. External public data represents mainly worst-case losses, while losses from data-sharing initiatives presumably cover the middle range of a loss distribution.

As explained in detail within "Economic and regulatory capital" later in the chapter, the trend at many banks diverts from the use of external data in the sense of data points in a distribution. Rather, a number of banks are moving towards using such external data as a starting point for their own scenario analysis, which can take into account the individual bank's circumstances with regard to products, process, systems, locations and so forth.

Scenario analysis

As described in the previous section, rare major losses are important for an adequate evaluation of risk potential, but hard to obtain. Internal data reflects such losses only to a small extent, and external data relates to possibly fundamentally different circumstances in the institutions involved (differences as to products, processes, systems and staff, and their consistent categorisation).

The attempt is therefore made to cover rare major losses not, or at least not exclusively, with historical data, but through structured analysis and evaluation of risky situations with risk potential. This approach is known as scenario analysis.

A similar approach is used for preparing strategic decisions, in particular in industrial areas, where possible future scenarios are worked out and examined as to the likelihood of their occurrence and resulting monetary consequences, eg, with respect to the evolution of sales possibilities and the behaviour of competitors. A well-known technique of this type is the Delphi method, with which statements are extracted by the structured, multilevel questioning of teams of experts. Scenario analysis can, depending on the concrete methodology employed, have close points of contact with risk assessments (see "Risk assessment" in this chapter).

A decision is taken as to whether best-case, likely-case or worst-case scenarios are to be the subject of the investigation. In the case of operational risk, worst-case scenarios are usually the focus.

The experience of financial institutions with scenario techniques has been limited up to now. A first step in scenario analysis can be the brainstorming of situations in which significant risks are presumed (eg, the breakdown of critical systems, unavailability of a large number of employees, terrorist attack). The categorisation of events can thereby serve as a helpful starting point for such investigations. Furthermore, both internal losses and external data can be used as sources of information. One example of this is the analysis of the consequences of a short-time system breakdown, and, based on this, a forecast of whether this event would have led to significant losses if it had lasted longer. Another starting point for scenario analysis can be near misses.

The next step is concerned with specifying the situation to such an extent that an expert judgement can be made as to the likelihood of occurrence and the size of potential losses. In certain circumstances it may be necessary beforehand to filter redundant situations or ones that are irrelevant to the examination from the result of the brainstorming, so as not to endanger the efficiency of the evaluation. In the system-breakdown case it must be determined, among other things, which systems are assumed to break down, how long a breakdown lasts and which applications, products and processes are affected.

The scenarios are subsequently evaluated – an analysis is made of the frequency of occurrence and an estimate of the size of loss associated with the occurrence.

Finally, the scenarios and their evaluation must be validated, or at least made plausible. To do this, a panel of experts who did not participate in specifying and evaluating the scenarios could undertake an independent evaluation, eg, the subject of their investigation is both the completeness and relevance of the scenarios selected with a view to covering all significant risks and also the validity or plausibility of the results of the evaluation.

In addition to the estimation of frequency and the size of individual loss events described above, the interdependence of the occurrence of different loss events could be the subject of scenario analysis. This can serve to derive correlation assumptions, which play a role in the quantification of operational risk.

RISK ASSESSMENT

Risk assessment describes a method or programme aimed at the qualitative assessment and evaluation of operational risk. Even though the result may be numeric, the assessment is based on subjective estimates by individuals or groups. The result cannot be objectively observed, measured or derived, unlike loss data or indicators.

Other designations are "self-assessment", "risk self-assessment", "risk and control assessment" and so on. The different and to some extent not precisely defined concepts reflect different components or chief characteristics of a risk assessment, such as areas or scope of analysis or evaluation, implementation methods and participants.

Thus, even though no norms or general standards for risk assessments exist, they are considered to be a form of scenario analysis that has been simplified through structuring questions along a framework of categories and clustering answers according to a strict scheme of potential results. Risk assessments are carried out by financial institutions in vastly different forms, but there are, as yet, no standards. Examples of approaches include:

- Simple question lists on risk complexes or individual risks;
- questionnaires on risk-mitigating measures (such as controls);
- assessment of risk potential (often by both likelihood and severity);
- scenario analysis;
- scorecards; and
- combinations of the above.

For the purpose of this book, the expression "risk assessments" will be used as a generic term for all forms of such assessments. Special designations will be only used where they highlight specific elements of the method concerned.

Risk assessments aim at identification and qualitative evaluation of operational risk in a forward looking manner. The aims they pursue include:

- identification of those risks that are relevant for the institution, the business line or the department;
- evaluation of the potential for loss on occurrence of identified risks;
- evaluation of the likelihood of the occurrence of identified risks;
- evaluation of the quality of controls per process, organisational unit or the entire risk management process;
- analysis of weak points in organisations, processes and systems;
- description of the institutions' risk situation for management and control purposes;
- definition of future risk mitigation measures; and
- awareness building for staff to detect operational risk.

Risk assessments are characterised by four essential components or distinguishing features:

- type of risks and controls: the risks and controls to be assessed;
- object and scope: the components that classify the objects of evaluation from an organisational or other point of view;
- evaluation yardstick: the dimension which is used to categorise or cluster the results; and
- evaluation form: describes whether evaluated objects lie in its sphere of influence or not.

Types of risk and controls

The risks as the elements of a risk assessment can be evaluated either on a net or gross basis and can also include existing controls.

Net or residual risks are those risks whose occurrence is measured taking into account all existing and relevant risk mitigating measures or controls. They represent a consciously realistic evaluation of the current risk potential, taking into account all existing risk management measures. These can include process inherent, preventive or detective controls, or risk mitigation on a higher level such as insurance or business continuity management. The evaluation must take these into account in their state at time of evaluation. Sometimes, a distinction is made here between an evaluation taking into account the actual risk-mitigating measures including possible defects and an evaluation assuming measures operating under ideal conditions. The assessment is usually done either in a kind of free form, where potential risks are identified and later structured for management purposes or based on a predefined inventory of all risks considered relevant.

To ensure a certain level of consistency, it has proven useful to perform the assessment based on the matrix defined earlier as described in the section on definitions and structures of observation.

Gross or inherent risks tend to be theoretical objects of evaluation, as they are in reality mainly not observable directly, as most of them are already mitigated by a pre-existing system of controls, such as backup systems, insurance and so on. Nevertheless, their identification and evaluation is a useful and often necessary step in risk assessment. Only such an analysis can make explicit the actual exposure to risk of an activity, a business unit or a product and demonstrates the extent to which risk management is dependent on controls in this area. Also, only an assessment of gross risks allows a well-founded decision on cutting back measures that have been recognised as ineffective.

If two processes, products or business units display the same risk from the net point of view, but not from the gross point of view, the extent to which both are dependent on the successful operation of existing measures becomes evident. Both their identification and their evaluation require powers of abstraction, as they are investigated under explicit exclusion of all risk-mitigation measures.

As a third object of a risk assessment after gross and net risks, controls or risk-mitigating measures need to be evaluated. This enables an assessment of their suitability for mitigating a risk. In doing so, they may be categorised as preventive or detective controls such as, eg, a second person looking at a transaction, physical-access controls for a building or a fire detector. It is however useful to focus not just on inherent controls. For a comprehensive risk profile all measures need to be taken into account. This includes more remote risk management measures or high level controls such as the quality of outsourcing management, business continuity management and insurance programmes. How such controls should be included in an assessment depends on two aspects. The first aspect refers to management's ability to actually control a measure directly, indirectly or not at all, whereas the other aspect refers to the management's knowledge about the existence of the control at all. In practice there is for example, at group and department level – and frequently also at the business line level – a certain lack of knowledge concerning insurance programmes and the concrete coverage they provide. The decision concerning buying such coverage often also does not lie at the same management level. Consequently, any assessment done by the management of a certain

Figure 25 Relationship between gross risks, net risks and controls

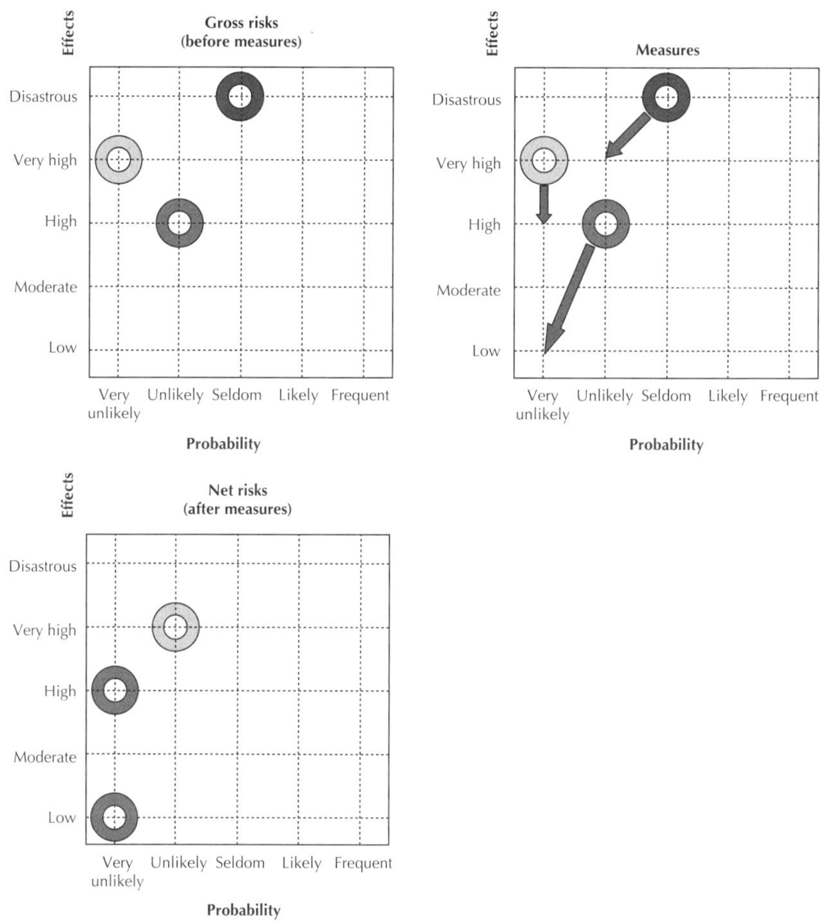

unit without full knowledge of existing high level controls will lead to an overrating of the net or residual risk. For a comprehensive and more realistic result, those responsible for high level controls need to be involved. Over time, management will gain a better knowledge about these controls, and sometimes even power to make decisions, so that in the long run they will gain a better understanding of the complete risk profile of their organisational unit.

Object and scope of the assessment

Object and scope of an assessment describe the area from an organisational or logical point of view where an assessment of the risks is to be made.

The objects of evaluation in a risk assessment programme can be processes or parts thereof, organisational units or products, but also any other level that can be delineated from the organisational point of view, such as legal entity, branch office or geographical unit.

Objects of an assessment should be selected in such a way that they include all relevant or key areas to be examined and at the same time provide the greatest level of practicability. As with any analysis, there exists a trade-off between information needs and the effort necessary to obtain such information. It may be desirable to include all subsidiaries however remote they may be from the risk point of view – eg, because of its scope – yet conducting an assessment might not be in an annual risk assessment, from a cost perspective it may not be feasible, or only with considerable difficulty.

The process view

A prominent example of this is the assessment of processes rather than organisational units. Processes provide a considerable advantage over most other objects of evaluation: they include, along the flow of the bank's value chain, all relevant risks as well as any controls that exist in an objectively logical context. A pure and complete process view of an institution omits no relevant aspect and includes in particular areas of high risk such as interfaces between units.

Using processes as the object of subsequent evaluation makes an unambiguous attribution of risks to the processes concerned possible. One major advantage is seen in the fact that possible improvements to the process are directly attributable, both in their effects and in their costs. One major disadvantage however that should not be overlooked is that, because of the great complexity of banks today with their large numbers of processes, there is seldom any complete and up-to-date end to end documentation of them. Frequently, a project tries to implement a uniform documentation across the entire bank. In general, only a few areas are documented completely and up-to-date. Owing to the complexity of this undertaking and the time involved, organisational changes often take place more quickly than their documentation. Thus it is seldom possible to have recourse to appropriate process descriptions for the purposes of a risk assessment.

A process description specifically for the purposes of a risk assessment, less detailed in non-risk relevant aspects, would seem to be an alternative. However, since such a description would also have to deal with similar problems as described above, it can be carried out only with the commitment of considerable resources. Complete documentation of risks, controls, interfaces and their consequences is thus in practice achievable only with considerable effort. Moreover, the so-called "process owner" principle is known to only a few organisations – there is seldom one person responsible for a process with clearly defined responsibilities. Usually processes extend over several organisational units and thus several separate areas of responsibility. This renders the attribution of risks, management decisions, and costs and effects more difficult.

Choosing processes as the main object of an assessment, however conceptually superior as it may seem, often is not feasible within bigger organisations due to complexity involved.

The product view

The product concept is closely related to the process view and thus shares many of its advantages and disadvantages. Choosing products, not the value chain, is within the focus of an assessment, but is overall the result of a chain. As in the case of the process view, the result of a complete coverage according to products provides an almost complete picture of an organisation. This perspective allows direct attribution of the risks to the product produced. This supports the exact determination of costs of risk management at product level. However, the attribution of central support and service units remains problematic. Such units do not create products in the sense they are usually understood to, but mainly services. Another problem arises from the assignment of management responsibility to products. Product responsibility from the first step of creation up to the internal or external sale of the product is seldom found. Moreover, different products are not infrequently produced in the same units or during the same or similar process steps. A clear and unambiguous attribution of the operational risk inherent there is thus very difficult. Correspondingly, the risks identified and the risk-mitigating measures or controls cannot be attributed to products in all cases.

Therefore products seem attractive as the object of a risk assessment at first glance, but problems mainly around the roles and responsibilities of all functions involved in creating them make it very difficult to adequately attribute assessments of risk and control.

The organisational view

Organisational units such as teams, departments and business units allow for a complete observation of all operational risks within an organisational unit – which usually also coincides with a clearly delineated area of responsibility. A significant advantage of these objects for observation is the clear assignment of responsibility. Those responsible for the management of an organisational unit usually also have the control over the risk mitigating measures. Essential disadvantages of this perspective for observation lie in particular in the treatment of operational risk that arises at interfaces to other units, which are a considerable source. Thus, completeness of documentation can be achieved – with considerable limitations – only through the cooperation of several areas. A direct assignment to processes and products is possible only to a limited extent, and the corresponding derivation of the risk costs associated therewith accordingly difficult.

Nevertheless, this level of observation has gained acceptance by most banks for two reasons. For one thing, organisational units exist already independently of all efforts to manage operational risk. Thus the documentation and demarcation of these topics of evaluation pose no additional requirements on the bank. Secondly, there is as a rule a clear management responsibility for organisational units, integrated into a hierarchical system with superior and subordinate levels of responsibility, which facilitates the implementation of risk mitigation measures. The identity of observation

Table 7 Comparison of different risk assessment perspectives

Object and scope	Suitable for	Pro	Contra
Processes	Strongly process-oriented organisations with few core processes or many similar processes capable of being standardised	Complete mapping of a value chain	In the absence of a process-owner concept unclear assignment of management responsibility
Products	Strongly product-driven organisations with few support units or processes with small risk content	Complete mapping of a product or group of products	Problems with heterogeneous products, high service component and many support units with unclear product definition
Organisational units	Conventionally structured banks with business lines, central management areas and service areas	Clear assignment of management responsibility	Problems with capture of interfaces that experience has shown to be highly fraught with risks

object and management responsibility can therefore be considered the major advantage of this perspective.

Structure of observation
A risk assessment can be undertaken free of any structure or categorising. However, in order to make comparisons possible, whether over time, against peers or a desired state, the use of a consistent structure is recommended. This can be the risk categorisation used by the bank, a more detailed or simplified version or some other, different categorisation.

To facilitate the integration of risk assessment into the overall operational risk management concept, but in particular to allow a reconciliation with the other measurement or evaluation procedures such as loss data, indicators and VaR, the use of a consistent structure for observation of all elements of the framework seems the obvious choice (see "Definitions and structures" in this chapter).

Evaluation yardstick
As the risks to be evaluated in a risk assessment do not possess a measurable dimension in the sense of an objectively determinable condition, they may be evaluated according to a variety of yardsticks. The evaluation can thereby be performed in one or two dimensions. In the case of gross and net risks, usually impact and likelihood will be assessed. Evaluation of control quality either takes place in one single dimension or with simultaneous evaluation of their efficiency and/or effectiveness. Both risks and controls are usually evaluated in discrete form using multilevel scales with ranges.

Effects
In the case of gross and net risks, the evaluation of the possible effects represents an attempt to estimate the level of loss upon occurrence of a certain risk event. This can be expressed in the form of absolute values or of ranges or in relation with other indicators such as turnover, number of transactions or employees. Absolute values facilitate aggregation of risk information on all levels of a bank, as well as the comparison of such results across similar units. Relative values, on the other hand, make comparisons easier,

Figure 26 Effects, probability and management measures

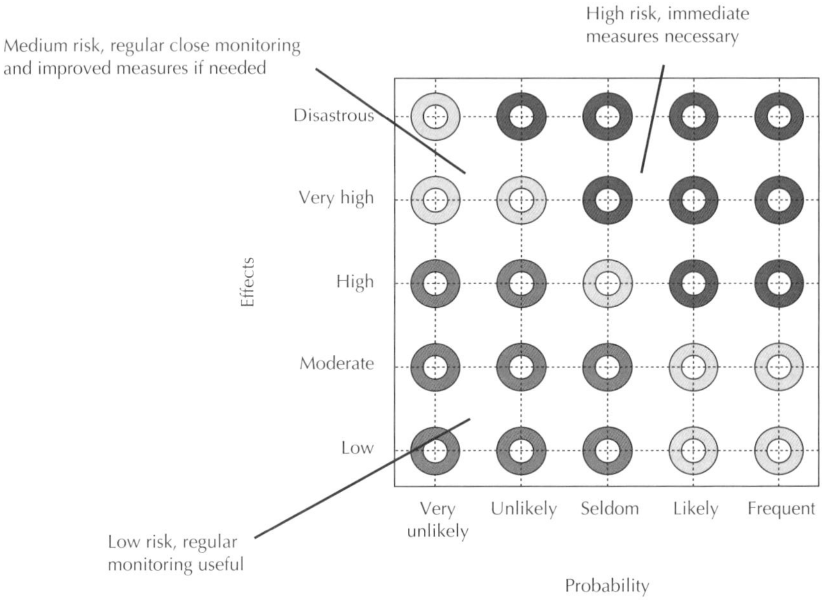

when, for example, statements are to be made concerning the exposure to risk of individual areas and their risk taking capacity.

The number of levels or ranges that should be used for the evaluation depends on aspects specific to each bank. There exists no uniformly applicable scale.

If a particular number of levels are already familiar from other risk areas, it may make sense to use them for the purposes of an operational risk assessment as well, in order to retain a certain consistency and continuity in reporting results. Experience has shown that, in the case of assessments, use is seldom made of more than ten levels. Many banks use a reduced, five-level scale. However, in the case of scales with an uneven number there is a tendency to choose the middle value in every case where there are no compelling reasons for a different assessment. This avoids a negative or positive assessment from the point of view of the user of such scales. An even number does not allow for this and each assessment has to have a clearly positive or negative result. Which approach to select depends on the above mentioned aspects.

Several aspects are important for the decision whether to use an absolute or a relative scale such as the primary recipient, the assessment goal and the manner of any possible further processing of the results. If the risk is to be considered from the point of view of the entire bank with emphasis on material and major loss potentials, the use of an absolute scale makes sense. This standardises the results from all areas by making use of a uniform yardstick, mainly a financial one expressed in currency terms. From the overall organisation's point of view, this enables the relevant risks to be identified quickly across all areas, aggregated and correspondingly addressed.

On the other hand, a relative scale supplies information specific to the business line involved, which makes the relative risks of the unit under observation clearer. At the overall bank level, a relative scale allows for the easy identification of larger risk potentials in individual business lines. This can be of great importance, in particular when the absolute risk of a business line is small from the overall bank view, but the proper functioning of this business line is of high relevance to the entire institution.

When deciding on a scale, the values or ranges must be selected in such a way that the primary goal can be reached. If the emphasis is placed on identifying material risks that threaten the going concern of the entire bank, the selection of adequately large values is recommended. The highest range should be unlimited, since the maximum risk in the event of a disaster corresponds to the value of the bank in liquidation. However, for meaningful evaluations in the area of large and very large risks, the ranges below this should not be selected too high, in order to obtain results in these areas. At medium to large banks, a range limit for overall bank risk assessments of €50 million or more is frequently used, while the lower limits are mainly in the region of €50,000 to €100,000. But these values frequently appear too high at the business line level. There are, as mentioned, no generally applicable rules for defining the upper and lower limits. As a general guide, the upper limit can be set to a figure at which a threat to the continued existence of the unit under observation occurs. Conversely, the lower limit should be selected such that the value does not represent a insignificant amount.

Scales that allow for a business line view with lower values and an overall bank view with higher values corresponding to the

Figure 27 Alternative approaches to aggregation of risk assessments

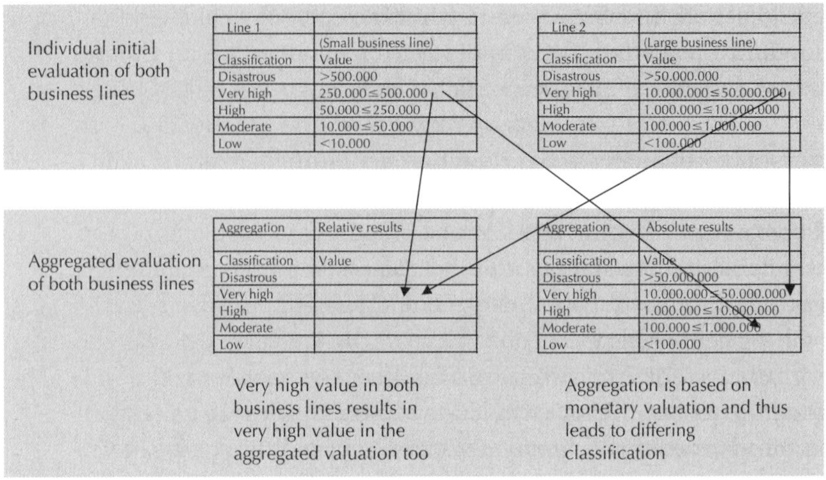

threat to continued existence do justice to both aims. However, these presuppose corresponding rules for aggregating the results. There exist basically two different approaches:

- ❑ aggregation of the corresponding values (the absolute figures); and
- ❑ aggregation of the individual business lines or levels of the specific scales.

Combining the values allows for aggregation ie, desirable from the point of view of the entire bank. The recipient of the results can compare the absolute level of risk; simple aggregations across several units and levels are possible, because of the uniform use of absolute amounts. However, in the course of aggregation, information on risks relevant to the individual business lines may be lost. Values that are too small from the point of view of the bank as a whole, but of fundamental significance for the individual business line, are no longer identifiable as such once aggregated to the next organisational level.

Aggregation of the individual ranges or level values retains this information. For example, the maximum value of one business line is transferred to the maximum level in the evaluation of the bank as a whole.

Whereas aggregation of absolute values leads to a total result for the entire bank, aggregation of the value ranges leads to a summarised presentation of the risk profiles.

Probability

The estimation of probability is aimed at assessing the frequency of an occurrence. With regard to different evaluation approaches, the statements concerning the impacts apply – *mutatis mutandis* – to the assessment of the probability of an event. The valuation can be made here, too, in ranges or with point values; the scales can be absolute or relative and can consist of an even or uneven number of values. Likewise there are similar problems with totalling or aggregating the results.

The ranges to be selected also depend essentially on the purpose of the assessment or the time frame. In the case of regularly conducted risk assessments, for example, on an annual basis, a five-level scale is frequently used by many organisations, covering periods from quarterly, as a lower limit, to five to ten or more years, as an upper limit.

Where other aims are in view, these can be adjusted accordingly. For example, if within the framework of a merger or outsourcing project, possible risks until completion of the transaction or for a defined period are to be determined, it would be sensible to adjust the scale used accordingly. Depending on the anticipated risks, the lower limit selected could also be a week, or occasionally a day. An upper limit corresponding to the period of the transaction or a slighter longer period would make sense.

Table 8 Examples of frequency ranges for risk assessments

Frequency	Very unlikely	Unlikely	Seldom	Likely	Frequent
Long-term observation/ annual analysis	More seldom than every 10 years	Every 5–10 years	Every 1–5 years	Annually	Quarterly
Short-term observation	Annually or more seldom	Half-yearly or more seldom	Quarterly or more seldom	Monthly or more seldom	Weekly or more seldom

Control quality

As with effects and probability, within certain limits any suitable scale can be used for evaluating control quality. The same statements are also – *mutatis mutandis* – applicable here.

Control quality can be evaluated both by using a single dimension or a two-dimensional matrix. In the case of a two-dimensional evaluation, effectiveness and efficiency are evaluated. This has the advantage that, in addition to assessing the quality of a control in the narrower sense, the associated control costs – ie, the economic aspect – must also be explicitly assessed. This is based on the assumption that a risk is consciously taken and thus risk-mitigating measures should also not be established or maintained at any price. If this aspect is of no importance, such an evaluation can, as a consequence, be dispensed with. In the case of one-dimensional evaluation, an assessment of the effectiveness of a measure is most frequently focused upon, since this represents the more relevant aspect from the point of view of risk management. An economic component can be introduced here, too, if the scale for evaluation is complemented by this aspect in the area of good or very good controls. Unlike the assessment of effects and probability, it can be meaningful, when evaluating control quality, to assess, as a maximum attribute, the aspect of excessively good controls separately from the economic component. This is based on the assumption an error rate can increase again with the existence of excessively good controls, as too much confidence is placed in such controls and thus less care is taken in advance. Another rationale may be that the cost of control increases significantly when aiming for very

Figure 28 Examples of scales for the evaluation of control quality

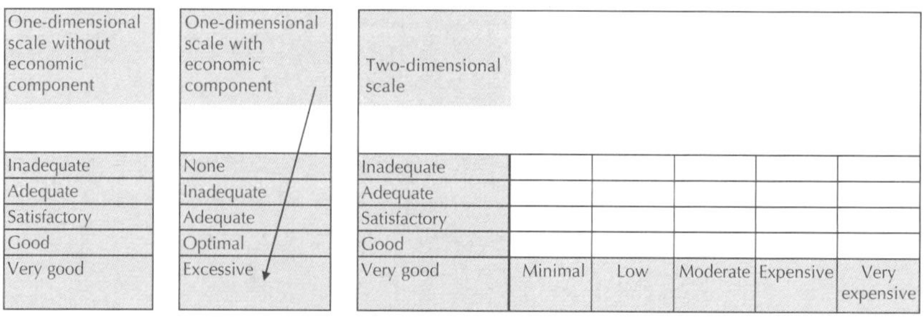

tight control and may become unjustifiable compared to the risks taken on from a certain level.

It is important to bear in mind when evaluating controls and in defining the evaluation scale to be used that the result of such an assessment does not equal automatically the difference between the gross and net risk. Controls can indeed affect both the impact and the probability, but they do so only rarely to the same extent.

Insurance, for example, does not influence the frequency of an event at all. However, it does limit the effects, once a payment has been initiated. Conversely, an independent duplicate capture of transactions can influence the frequency with which such transactions are entered incorrectly but not the effects, in the event that a false entry is made in both cases.

For this reason an explicit assessment of control quality is to be recommended in most cases. Only this provides transparency on the existing controls, on which are included in the evaluation and how good they are considered to be, and finally whether they make sense from an economic perspective.

Evaluation

Risk assessments can lastly be classified according to who performs them for an in scope object. The concept of "self" means in this respect that the evaluation of an object (eg, process, unit or product) is carried out by the person responsible for it – not by an independent third party. A major advantage of this approach is intimate knowledge of the object of analysis and its inherent risks. Disadvantages are the lack of objectivity and consequently the problems arising from comparing evaluations made by different individuals. In addition there is always the danger of consciously or unconsciously underestimating risks for two reasons: there may be a certain habitual blindness because of previous good or bad experience; and a tendency to assess risks in one's own area of responsibility as rather low, in fear of negative consequences.

These disadvantages can be offset only in part. A reconciliation of the results by an objective instance and the comparison with other available data such as loss data and indicators can be undertaken to reduce subjectivity. By definition neutral instances (such as a central risk control function) can be involved throughout the whole assessment process; and other independent functions possessing appropriate knowledge such as internal audit can be used to conduct regular or *ad hoc* reviews.

As an alternative approach, assessments can be carried out by independent parties. These can be persons external to the business line or to the enterprise. The corresponding advantages and disadvantages of an assessment by external persons are the opposite of those associated with assessments by internal persons. Whereas objectivity or habitual blindness will mostly not play a part, similarly exact knowledge of the individual risks will seldom be present, insofar as they are determined by the individual circumstances of a business line. However, these disadvantages are hardly present in the case of external risks such as natural disasters and the appraisal of external partners.

Problems in evaluating impact and probability

As discussed above, any assessment is usually conducted within a predefined framework providing among other guidelines a value scheme to use for estimating impact and likelihood. They are intended to ensure a certain consistency of valuation even when the evaluation is to be conducted by different persons and for different objects. This is to support – in addition to the individual valuation of business lines or departments – the comparison of different organisational units and an aggregation of these results. However, they do not obviate the problem of the subjectivity of the evaluation or a conscious misjudgement of risks. Such problems occur in different forms, depending on the approach used.

Approach

Because of the various options for structuring a risk assessment, no uniform way to perform one exists. However, it is possible to identify two fundamental approaches. It is thus possible to distinguish between risk assessments conducted in the form of a survey and those conducted within the framework of a workshop or a series of these.

In the case of a survey both in paper or computer-based form, individuals are asked independently of each other to assess defined risks in their area of responsibility, or for others. An essential feature of these is that the assessment takes place without the direct influence of other third parties providing their view during the process.

Figure 29 Alternative approaches to risk assessment

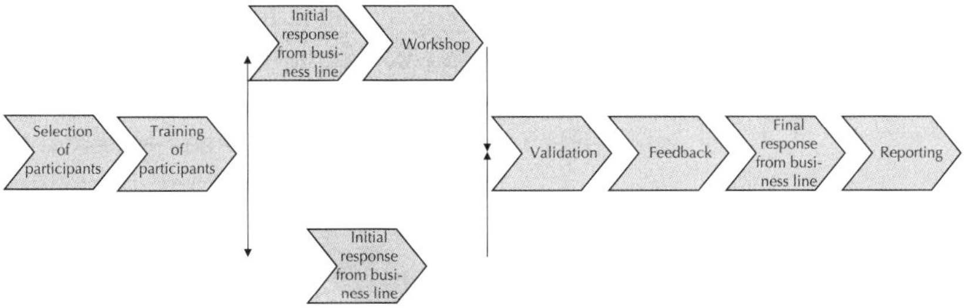

When the risk assessment is conducted in workshops, influence on the formation of the appraisers' opinion by other persons is consciously created. Each assessment or conclusion may be challenged or confirmed by other attendees, this providing an, if not independent but additional view.

There also exists the form of voting, which provides a combination of both approaches. It is often computer-supported, where everyone can see the individual or total results, but the individual voting or assessment behaviour of the participants remains anonymous.

There are options as to the point at where or how frequently feedback loops are built into the process. Owing to the high relevance of the results it seems – at the least – wise to implement one feedback loop, in order to enable in particular unpractised participants to correct their results in comparison with others. It is obvious that the process described runs in shorter form following repeated use. Participant selection and training are necessary and absolutely vital in the beginning, but for any follow up this is needed only in cases where new participants or new business lines are to be integrated into the risk assessment process.

Independently of the approach selected, the last step is attempting to reconcile or validate the results.

As risk assessment results are based on subjective assessments as described in detail, they need to be tested for plausibility. The reasons for this include:

- there is no incentive to provide a truthful but potentially negative assessment of their own area of responsibility;
- lack of experience of individual performing the assessment;

Table 9 Alternative approaches to risk assessment

Approach	Essential features	Pro/contra	Effort	Suitable for
Workshop	In general results identified in discussion over several hours, including a number of various areas and/or experts	Consciously induced levelling or standardisation of results through evaluation in discussion	Depending on extent, very resource heavy and time intensive	The evaluation of different areas, if a certain standardisation in approach and in particular in the application of valuation yardsticks cannot be ensured beforehand, since individual viewpoints can differ widely and/or specialist knowledge needs taking into account additionally
Survey	Individual, highly structured and, if necessary, anonymous questioning of individuals, can be on paper or electronic	Evaluation uninfluenced by third parties without possibility of correction or taking knowledge of others into account	Very efficient implementation, especially if computer-based	A rapid assessment, particularly if a certain standardisation in approach to and use of the valuation yardsticks is ensured

- ❑ lack of competence of individual performing the assessment;
- ❑ attitude of assessor to risk;
- ❑ recent and long term risk history;
- ❑ cross-area consistency of answers; and
- ❑ comparability of results over time.

Because of these problems inherent to any risk assessment, the results need to be reconciled, validated or at least tested as to plausibility by independent information. Depending on the kind of information available, this can take place in various ways. If a consistent structure for recording data exists, as described under "Definitions and structures" earlier in this chapter, it is relatively easy to compare the results of a risk assessment with loss data and indicators. Obviously, several time periods will have to pass until a reliable history has been built up, but the comparison of various data sources will still supply considerable information for plausibility purposes. The comparison of different business lines also contributes to this. Peer comparison, comparison over time or against a desired state, all provides information for the validation of risk assessment results.

A complete validation of risk assessment results is impossible, but essential aspects can be covered by different areas:

- risk control: cross-area consistency testing;
- internal audit: plausibility based on knowledge gained from audits;
- other data sources (such as loss data collection): consistency testing based on, for instance, historical losses, risk indicators; and
- benchmarking with competitors: comparison of risk profile with that of other institutions.

There are further variants of risk assessment, in theory as well as in practice. These are derived from the basic process described or variations thereof. The questionnaire or a workshop agenda can include, in addition to questions relevant for the entire bank, business line-specific ones too.

Such questions should cover the concrete and individual risks of a business line. The question of whether their analysis should be carried out in the form of the determination of impact and probability or by means of simple yes/no questions is secondary. Of greater importance is that these questions are defined in close cooperation between the business line affected and the unit compiling them.

Since such questions have by definition no relevance to other business lines, a different procedure must be used for determining the total result than the aggregation mechanisms described. As in the case of risk indicators (see "Key risk indicators" below), this can be achieved by transferring the results to a "traffic-light" system. Moreover, because of the degree of concreteness, they tend to lend themselves easily to a direct connection with indicators. If it is possible to link business line-specific questions with objective values, a considerable step towards validation will have been taken.

Figure 30 The aggregation of several risk assessment components

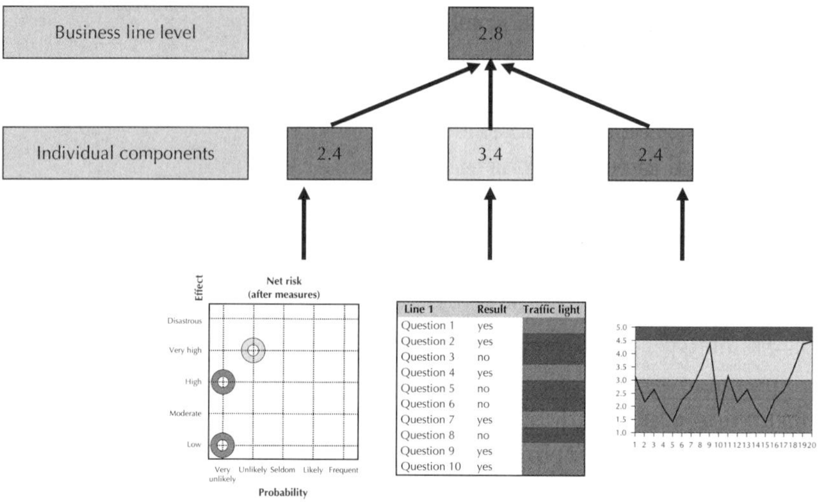

Depending on the addressee and the number of different information sources to be integrated, the final form of reporting can be determined. If feedback from the business line involved is foremost, communication of the results in an as uncondensed form as possible is preferable. If at least one of the aims is to determine a condensed result per business line, then aggregation is inevitable. To achieve this, the results of both or all three risk assessment components can be transferred to a consistent value scale, eg a "traffic-light" system.

KEY RISK INDICATORS

A central task of operational risk management is the early recognition of changes in a risk potential that can lead to losses. The aim here is to take measures that prevent the occurrence of losses with a high degree of probability. Such systems are known as early warning systems. They are mainly based on key risk indicators (KRIs).

KRIs are ratios that are capable of providing information about factors that determine risk. A key requirement of such risk indicators is the provision of *ex ante* information (a warning concerning future losses) instead of *ex post* information on losses that have already occurred (such as is gathered by the collection of loss data (see "Loss data" in this chapter).

Figure 31 Steps in a risk indicator model

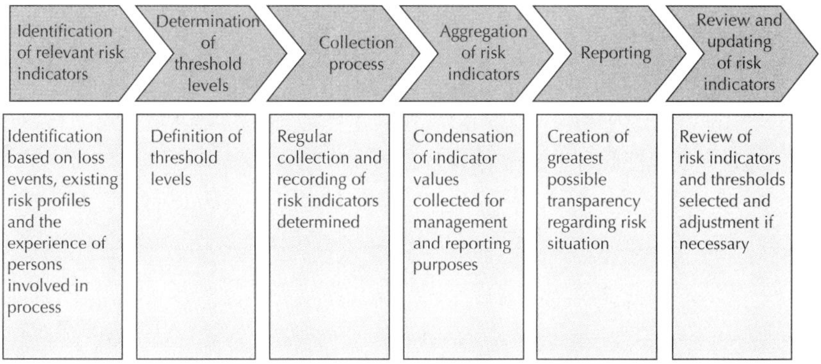

At the conceptual level, some banks equate risk indicators with key performance indicators (KPIs). The problem here is that KPIs are already well established instruments, in particular in production and IT areas, and which, as a rule, represent *ex post* measures relating to processes (load factors, throughput, error rate and similar). In individual cases a KPI can indeed be helpful in defining risk indicators; however, equating the two instruments is not advisable, because of the rather backward-looking character.

Identification

The first step in designing a risk indicator method consists of identifying suitable indicators. Particularly helpful here is the knowledge of the employees involved in the processes in the individual business lines. Brainstorming the possible determinants of the various risk categories in a small group has proven useful. The most important criterion for the suitability of ratios as risk indicators is their early warning character. For example, a count of pending lawsuits is useful only when an increase in this count is accompanied by an increase in the number of actual losses. Risk management must be directed towards the avoidance of future lawsuits (eg, by training employees so as to avoid advising errors); conversely, lawsuits already in existence can usually no longer be effectively influenced in the sense of risk management. Frequently, suitable risk indicators can be derived only from the linking of several ratios. Risk ensues, for example, from low employee availability (be it due to terminations, illness or annual holidays) only if the amount of work to be processed is simultaneously high and thus impending bottlenecks have to be cushioned, eg, by temporary staff.

Furthermore, relevance for management is dependent on the possibility of deriving concrete measures. Risk indicators that characterise situations that lie outside the sphere of influence of the bank tend to be unsuitable. And, finally, data availability aspects with regard to collection effort impose further requirements on the ratios. In the case of information not at present available in usable form, evaluation must be made from the cost–benefit point of view of whether determination is to be strived for in the future. Risk indicators can relate to individual processes, individual business lines or all business lines of the entire bank. The comparability is increased by a higher degree of standardisation across all business lines, but at the same time the possibility of individual risk management is reduced. Several attempts are being made at present to determine standardised risk indicators across banks.

Specification

Following identification, the risk indicators must be defined unambiguously (determination of the units). Many ratios permit leeway in their definition and/or can be obtained by the calculation of averages over several periods. There is also often a choice between planned and actual values for the calculation of corresponding ratios (eg, planned or approved or occupied job positions). It must further be defined who is responsible for collecting the risk indicators and how frequently this is to be done. Special departments such as human resources and legal will typically possess selected ratios for the bank as a whole, while process-oriented information from the back office is available only there and thus must be collected from the business line concerned.

Definition of threshold values

The next step is to determine which values of the risk indicator are uncritical, from which threshold a warning signal should be triggered that should lead to a review of the situation and to the launching of measures, and also a threshold at which an alarm should be triggered that must necessarily entail immediate measures.

Figure 32 Threshold values for risk indicators

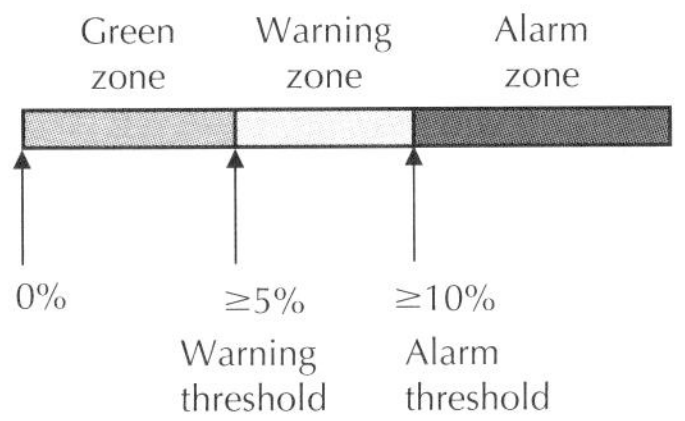

When determining such thresholds, the risk appetite of the individual decision maker is important, in addition to the experience of the experts involved. Warning and alarm signals that are regularly interpreted as false alarms, since the constellation that triggers them off is not seen as a risk situation, harm the acceptance of such a system to a considerable degree. "Traffic-light" systems have proved useful in this context, since they enable, at a glance, the statement whether a need for action is given or not. Moreover, it can be useful, in particular for aggregation purposes, to introduce, in addition to the rather coarse-grained classification into traffic-light colours, a more fine-grained ordinal or metric scale ie, independent of the units of the individual risk indicators. For this purpose, the deviation of the actual value of a risk indicator from the fixed threshold values can be evaluated mathematically. A linear function suffices for this in the simplest, most pragmatic case; individual banks have implemented more complex methods, such as fuzzy logic.

In addition to the one-sided risk indicators described, according to which an increase or decrease in the value of an indicator points monotonously to an increase in the risk content, two-sided risk indicators are also conceivable, according to which the optimal value lies within a range and thus both smaller and larger indicator values point to higher risks. This could be the case with the rate of staff utilisation in certain business lines, as experience shows that both permanent overworking and permanent scarcity of work can cause difficulties of concentration and thus increase proneness to errors. However, such indicators are seldom met in practice. Frequently only one direction of the indicator value points to a risk, while a movement in the opposite direction merely indicates inefficiency. Thus, too great a degree of utilisation of an IT system expresses a risk (that future transaction volumes can no longer be processed, insofar as they continue to increase), while too low utilisation ratios indicate redundancies in the system configuration, naturally giving rise to higher costs but not to a risk.

Collection process

Regular collection is necessary for the implementation of a risk-indicator system. Some banks have constructed corresponding systems that enable a direct connection to supplier systems and thus theoretically the determination of risk-indicator ratings on a daily basis. However, it has frequently become evident that most of the ratios needed can be determined just on a monthly basis or even less frequently. On the other hand, the costs of constructing the appropriate interfaces for the multitude of possible supplier systems that are usually available in banks are immense, whereas the benefit is dubious.

Thus, most financial institutions, meanwhile, rely on an at least semi-manual (and mostly monthly) collection process by which part of the information is collected from supplier systems by appropriate database queries, further processed in spreadsheets if required and entered into a suitable software tool (see "Risk Information Technology" below). Additional data is entered into the corresponding system from lists or reports that were prepared for other purposes. Thus, out of a balance between the topicalities of the information on the one hand and collection effort on the

Figure 33 Aggregation mechanism for risk indicators

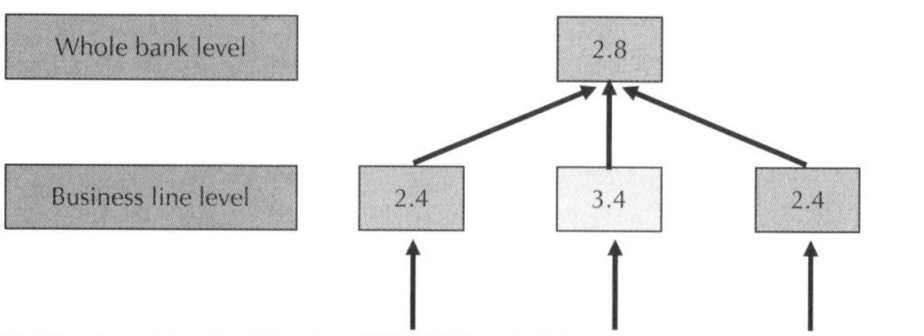

		Business line 1	Business line 2	Business line 3
Process	Weighting			
Cancellation rate	3	2.90	4.20	2.90
Complaints	2	1.90	2.90	2.90
Fluctuation	2	2.10	2.80	1.20

other, the monthly performance of such a collection process has crystallised as being the most widespread. Depending on the concrete content and the degree of granularity, collection in a centralised or decentralised manner can make sense. In any event, a centralised quality assurance ie, capable of recognising errors in collecting, is of major importance.

Aggregation

An aggregation of the individual indicators at the level of the business line or entire bank is necessary for reporting purposes. The main problem with aggregation is that the early warning character of the system suffers from the condensing of information. It is thus not suitable to permit a large number of green lights to dominate single red lights, leading to the reporting of a supposedly risk-free situation. It is therefore expedient – in addition, eg, to weighted mean values – to introduce rules that ensure the dominance of red and also amber lights, as necessary. For example, a mechanism similar to the school promotion system could be established that ensures, in spite of an arithmetically good mean value, that, in the presence of a certain number of red and/or amber lights, a red traffic light will be displayed, ie, in cases where the corresponding indicators point to areas of considerable risk.

Reporting

Finally, a reporting system (see also "Management information system" below) should ensure that the relevant decision makers are supplied with suitable information for deducing corresponding measures. It seems thereby advisable to depict, in addition to the relevant current values, the historical development – both for individual indicators and for an aggregated view – so that trends can be recognised. This would in individual cases permit measures to be taken before the amber zone is reached – eg, when a trend within the green zone in the direction of the amber zone is present. Conversely, it is easier to decide whether a currently amber or red traffic light represents an outlier or a systematic deterioration.

Updating

Risk indicator systems need to be examined regularly as to their suitability against the background of accumulated experience. It

Figure 34 Reporting system for risk indicators

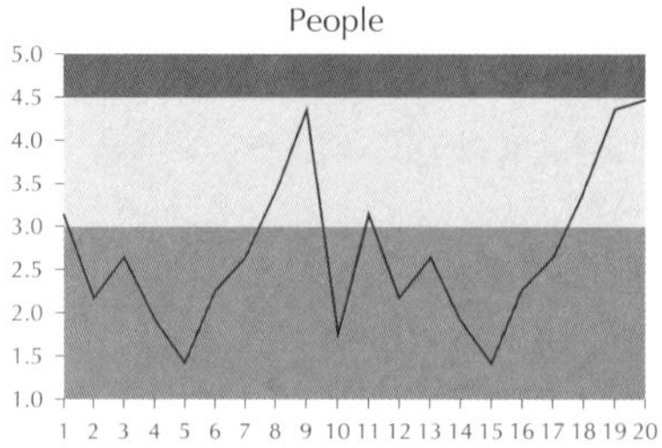

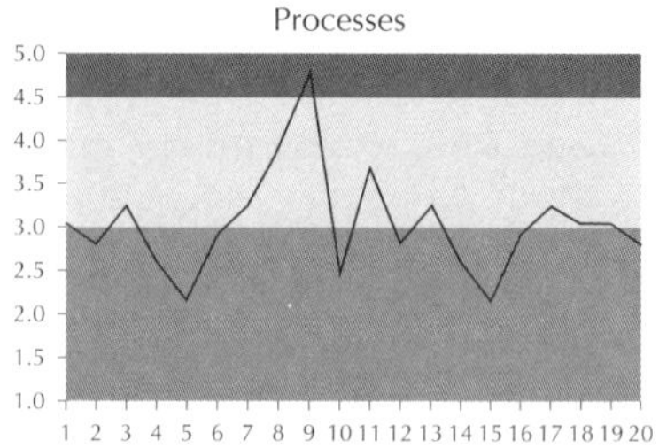

Persons				
KRI	Weight-ing	Current Value	Prior period	Prior period-1
Termination rate	3	4.7	4.5	4.4
Employee without longer holidays	1	4.9	4.9	4.9
Unauthorised system access	2	4.0	3.0	3.0
Aggregation		4.5	4.1	4.0

Processes				
KRI	Weight-ing	Current Value	Prior period	Prior period-1
Change request	2	2.5	2.5	2.5
Fluctuation rate	2	3.5	3.7	3.7
Cancellation rate	3	2.1	3.1	3.0
Open items	2	3.7	3.0	3.2
Aggregation		2.9	3.1	3.1

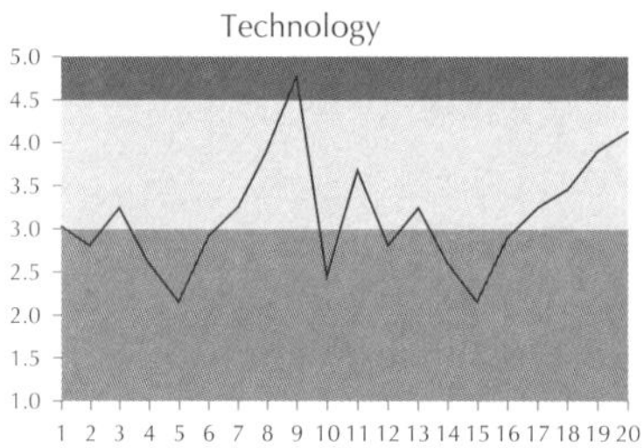

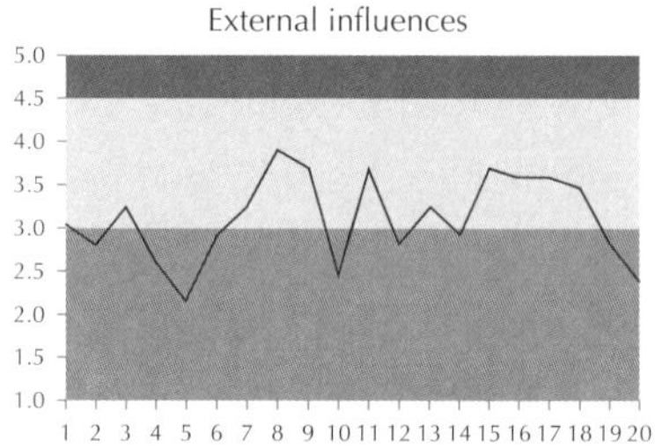

Technology				
KRI	Weight-ing	Current value	Prior period	Prior period-1
Hardware changes	1	1.4	1.9	2.0
Software changes	2	4.4	4.9	4.9
Virus attacks	3	4.7	3.9	3.0
Aggregation		4.1	3.9	3.5

External influences				
KRI	Weight-ing	Current value	Prior period	Prior period-1
Supplier with-out contract	2	2.0	3.3	5.0
Defective maintenance	1	1.9	1.6	1.9
Policy overrides	3	3.0	3.0	3.0
Aggregation		2.5	2.9	3.5

may be necessary to replace or adjust individual risk indicators or to modify the threshold values associated therewith. Ideally, a test of the effectiveness of the risk indicator system should be made by analysing correlation with losses incurred. Assuming that adequate measures were introduced on reaching red or amber traffic lights, it should be possible to observe a reduction in the number of losses incurred. The experience of some banks shows that such connections could be established in only very rare cases. The presumed reasons for this are manifold and could point to both an ineffective risk indicator system and a variety of further determinants that were not taken into account in the analysis.

One example of this is the ratio of temporary employees to permanent staff. It is intuitively assumed that an increase in the ratio leads to an increase in the error rate owing to poorly trained or less committed personnel and thus to a greater risk. In fact, it can often be observed in practice that the error rate actually falls. This could be attributed to more intensive checking of the work of such temporary workers by superiors. In this case, increased control effort must also be taken into account in analysing this indicator, as necessary. Obviously, difficulties in analysing indicators can signify both poor availability of data and simply insufficient experience of the interactions. It may be expected that the possibilities for analysis will improve in the course of time.

MANAGEMENT INFORMATION SYSTEM

The management information or reporting system as a component of a framework for operational risk management defines the flow of information between all components of this framework and between the suppliers and recipients of information involved. It is dependent on the type, number and scope of the other components of the framework that have been established. It includes a description of the overall aims, the actual reporting process, the roles and responsibilities of all employees involved and the technical implementation.

Aims and reporting process

The description of the overall aims of the management information system lays down what fundamental goals are to be achieved by it. These can range from reporting the day-to-day status of all risks to the board of directors, through the reporting only of events that exceed certain thresholds, down to the simple collection of data with a quarterly or semi-annually reporting cycle. Moreover, which information is given in what form and frequency to external recipients is defined here.

It is essential that all levels of the bank's management are adequately supported by the management information system, both as to content and as to processes. This presupposes appropriate procedures and methods for obtaining the information, robust and error-resistant arrangements for passing them on, and the knowledge necessary to interpret the results.

Whereas the indicators are generally well understood in the relevant business lines, since they make a direct statement concerning the condition of a process, their interpretation at an aggregated level is frequently more difficult. They must therefore be enriched by comparative data. Much the same applies to all components of the framework of operational risk management that supply or require information. Thus daily reporting of the VaR is possible, provided a corresponding quantification model is in existence. However, it is not advisable, since this value does not possess any relevance for the day-to-day operational risk management, because of its varied determinants and assumptions and also the usually annual frequency of determination.

Figure 35 Components of a management information system

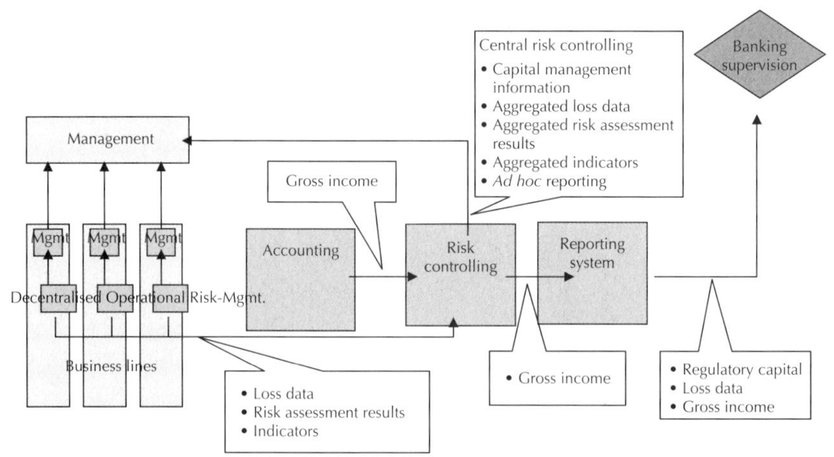

Roles and responsibilities

Only a clear definition of the roles and responsibilities present within the framework of the management information system ensures functioning reporting across all hierarchical levels and business lines of a bank. In addition to an initial separation according to suppliers and receivers of information, further differentiation of these tasks makes sense. Thus the recorders of loss data will only in rare cases be identical to those responsible for passing them on to centralised risk control. Within this process, a differentiation between the recording, reporting, quality control and passing on of loss data may be implemented within one business line, depending on the size of the units concerned and of the enterprise as a whole. Steps for further checks on quality or plausibility, appropriate consolidation and the passing on of information to the various recipients must be established within the central risk-control process.

Corresponding responsibilities for reacting to the information received (implementation of measures) must be defined for the recipients of reports. Type and scope should be differentiated here. A monthly loss data report to a risk committee will not be handled in the same way as an *ad hoc* report on an exposed embezzlement.

Technical implementation

The technical implementation must be oriented towards the requirements defined by the aims with regard to extent, type and structure, whereby there is considerable latitude concerning their concrete form. If the entire framework is still under construction, if the requirements are not defined in detail or if there is uncertainty concerning the approach to be selected, implementation on a short-term view can be conducted on the basis of standard office software.

It is essential that the conceptual necessities not be disregarded just because IT system support is not complete. In most cases manual steps are possible that should compensate for such deficiencies. This can be achieved by increased manual control steps even in areas in which a dual control principle or audit security is required. Only a few systems on offer today are endowed with the necessary flexibility needed in the construction phase of a framework. They also anticipate to a certain extent decisions regarding the methodology to be used. These can be corrected later only at great cost, for which there is little acceptance following a conception phase.

Figure 36 Example of a board report

Board report on operational risk

Date xx.xx.xx

News

Unusual loss events

Internal	1 xxxxxxxxxxxxxxxxxxxxxxxxxxxxxxxxxxxxxxx
	2 xxxxxxxxxxxxxxxxxxxxxxxxxxxxxxxxxxxxxxx
	3 xxxxxxxxxxxxxxxxxxxxxxxxxxxxxxxxxxxxxxx
External	1 xxxxxxxxxxxxxxxxxxxxxxxxxxxxxxxxxxxxxxx
	2 xxxxxxxxxxxxxxxxxxxxxxxxxxxxxxxxxxxxxxx
	3 xxxxxxxxxxxxxxxxxxxxxxxxxxxxxxxxxxxxxxx
Current developments Audit findings	xxxxxxxxxxxxxxxxxxxxxxxxxxxxxxxxxxxxxxx
Internal	none
External	xxxxxxxxxxxxxxxxxxxxxxxxxxxxxxxxxxxxxxx

Loss data

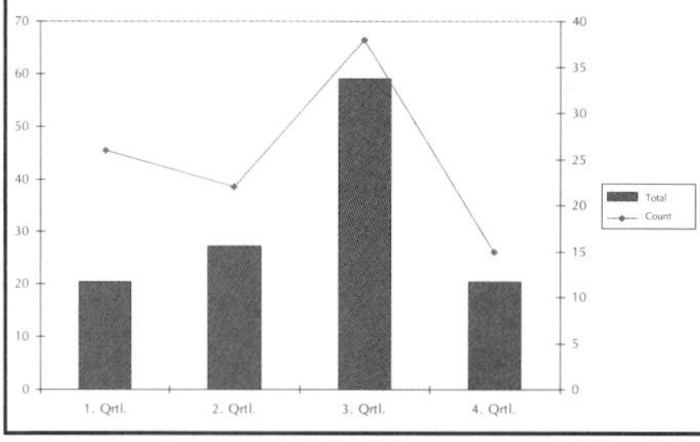

Top 10 events

1 xxxxxxxxxxxxxxxxxxxxxxxxxxxxxxxxxxxxxxx
2 xxxxxxxxxxxxxxxxxxxxxxxxxxxxxxxxxxxxxxx
3 xxxxxxxxxxxxxxxxxxxxxxxxxxxxxxxxxxxxxxx
4 xxxxxxxxxxxxxxxxxxxxxxxxxxxxxxxxxxxxxxx
5 xxxxxxxxxxxxxxxxxxxxxxxxxxxxxxxxxxxxxxx
6 xxxxxxxxxxxxxxxxxxxxxxxxxxxxxxxxxxxxxxx
7 xxxxxxxxxxxxxxxxxxxxxxxxxxxxxxxxxxxxxxx
8 xxxxxxxxxxxxxxxxxxxxxxxxxxxxxxxxxxxxxxx
9 xxxxxxxxxxxxxxxxxxxxxxxxxxxxxxxxxxxxxxx
10 xxxxxxxxxxxxxxxxxxxxxxxxxxxxxxxxxxxxxxx

Development of indicators

Comments xxxxxxxxxxxxxxxxxxxxxxxxxxxxxxxxxxxxxxx
xxxxxxxxxxxxxxxxxxxxxxxxxxxxxxxxxxxxxxx

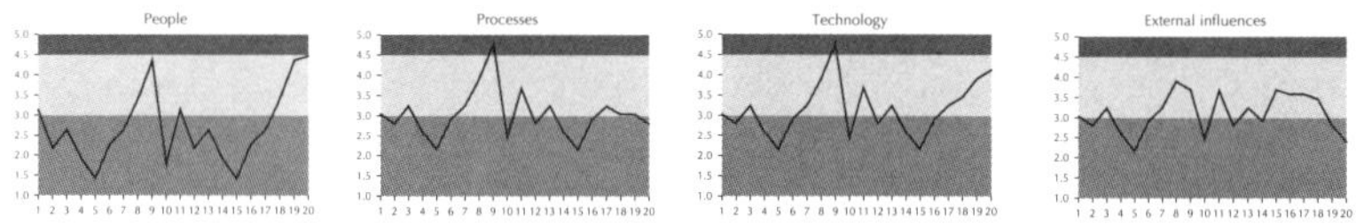

Persons				
KRI	Weighting	Current Value	Prior period	Prior period-1
Termination rate	3	4.7	4.5	4.4
Employee without longer holidays	1	[illegible]	[illegible]	[illegible]
Unauthorised system access	2	4.0	3.0	[illegible]
Aggregation		[illegible]	4.1	4.0

Processes				
KRI	Weighting	Current Value	Prior period	Prior period-1
Change request	2	2.5	2.5	2.5
Fluctuation rate	2	3.5	3.7	3.7
Cancellation rate	3	2.1	3.1	3.0
Open items	2	3.7	3.0	3.2
Aggregation		2.9	3.1	3.1

Technology				
KRI	Weighting	Current value	Prior period	Prior period-1
Hardware changes	1	1.4	1.9	2.0
Software changes	2	4.4	[illegible]	[illegible]
Virus attacks	3	4.7	3.9	3.0
Aggregation		4.1	3.9	3.5

External influences				
KRI	Weighting	Current value	Prior period	Prior period-1
Supplier without contract	2	[illegible]	3.3	[illegible]
Defective maintenance	1	1.9	1.6	1.9
Policy overrides	3	3.0	3.0	3.0
Aggregation		2.5	2.9	3.5

Risk assessment

Comments xxxxxxxxxxxxxxxxxxxxxxxxxxxxxxxxxxxxxxx
xxxxxxxxxxxxxxxxxxxxxxxxxxxxxxxxxxxxxxx

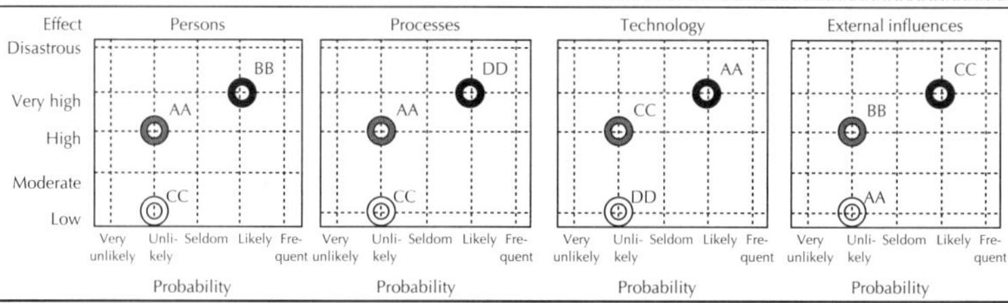

There are thus no ideal solutions for a management information system, but rather a balance should be sought between the necessary flexibility and acceptable increased manual effort. Relevant for risk management purposes are the informational content and its meaningful interpretation.

For example, reporting to the board of directors could therefore be designed as shown in Figure 36.

In addition to the presentation of current information, its relevance to management is material. Thus, such reporting could, as mentioned, include statements concerning economic and regulatory capital. However, since these will hardly change during the financial year, their presentation in a monthly report makes little sense. This may also be the case for other information. All reporting must therefore be regularly examined with regard to these requirements. It will be used only if it remains adequate for management purposes. Therefore, it is desirable, where possible, to integrate reporting on operational risk into an existing risk or management reporting system. Practice shows that too many reports and too much information will no longer be registered by the designated recipient. Examples of risk directors who read only the first page of an extensive risk report make this necessity clear. So emphasis should be placed on the summary and exception character. The need for detailed information arising from this can still be covered by a well-structured database and appropriate follow-up.

ECONOMIC AND REGULATORY CAPITAL

As previously mentioned, the banking supervisory authorities require, through the new Basel Capital Accord (Basel II) and the new Brussels Capital Requirements Directive (CRD), for the first time, the determination of regulatory capital for operational risk.

Even before discussion started on this topic, from about the mid-1990s onwards, individual internationally operating banks had made attempts to determine economic capital for operational risk. The need for this arises in particular from the consistent application of risk–reward management concepts (RAROC and others), which lead to undistorted decision support only when all material risk types are taken into consideration.

Initial attempts at measuring operational risk with models analogous to those used for the determination of the level of market or credit risk (eg, the internal measurement approach – IMA) have turned out to be rather disappointing. The reasons for this lie in the different nature of operational risk (primarily endogenous causes in contrast to the exogenous nature of market and credit risk events) and also in inadequate availability of data. An increase in complexity compared with market and credit risks results from the range of individual risks that are subsumed under the umbrella of operational risk (from erroneous entries of an employee through system breakdowns to natural disasters).

On the other hand, a look in the direction of other disciplines is more promising. Insurance companies, in particular reinsurance companies, have been entrusted for decades with the task of determining premiums for commercial insurance – such as that for fire and earthquake – with a similarly difficult data situation. Engineering science have conducted quantitative investigations for decades, particularly in applications in the aerospace and military areas, into the cause and probability of the failure of critical components and the resulting risks to the success of the mission.

Overview of quantification models

Quantification models can be characterised into top-down and bottom-up approaches, although the assignment to one of these categories is not always clear-cut.

Top-down approaches determine an economic or regulatory capital requirement at an aggregated level (generally the entire bank or group) and then distribute these to the individual units (business lines, departments and so on). Bottom-up approaches determine capital requirements for smaller units (business lines, departments) and aggregate the detailed results to an overall result for the entire bank or group.

While top-down approaches pose fewer requirements on the availability of data for the calculation, the development of a risk sensitive method for distributing the result to the individual units is difficult. On the other hand, bottom-up approaches require substantial numbers of high-quality data, and the aggregation of the detailed results is not trivial (taking correlations and portfolio effects into account).

Examples of top-down approaches are cost-based or earnings-based approaches (capital as a percentage of cost or earnings

Figure 37 Advantages and disadvantages of quantification approaches

Top-down	Bottom-up
• Relatively simple method of calculating a total figure for the bank or group • Barely risk-sensitive • Very difficult to break down to business lines • Few insights for management	• Supplies results for individual business lines etc. • Coverage of entire bank difficult • Relatively risk-sensitive • Detailed insights for management

figures), the Capital Asset Pricing Model method (stock market valuation as an indicator of operational risk) and the analysis of earnings volatility (earnings at risk). Common to all is the inadequate risk sensitivity of the measurement variable, which leaves in particular low-frequency, high-severity risks unaccounted for, since these are not adequately reflected in the measurement variables.

The majority of bottom-up approaches are based on historical loss data or expert estimates. These are mostly modelled via actuarial approaches that are also used for calculating premiums in the reinsurance business, partially making use of extreme value theory (EVT), so as to take into consideration low-frequency, high-severity losses explicitly.

Some banks regard top-down approaches as a "quick and dirty" entry into the topic of quantification, and then they are replaced with bottom-up approaches as the data situation improves and methodological knowledge develops further. The presentation below is focused on bottom-up approaches.

Bottom-up quantification models

In recent years, three classes of bottom-up approach have crystallised, and are currently regarded as being the most suitable:

- the loss-distribution approach (LDA);
- the scenario-based approach (ScA); and
- risk-drivers-and-controls approach (RDCA).

Individual banks have implemented these approaches in very different ways. The following description sketches core components of the individual approaches. Because of the fundamental

Figure 38 Connection between measurement, reporting and management

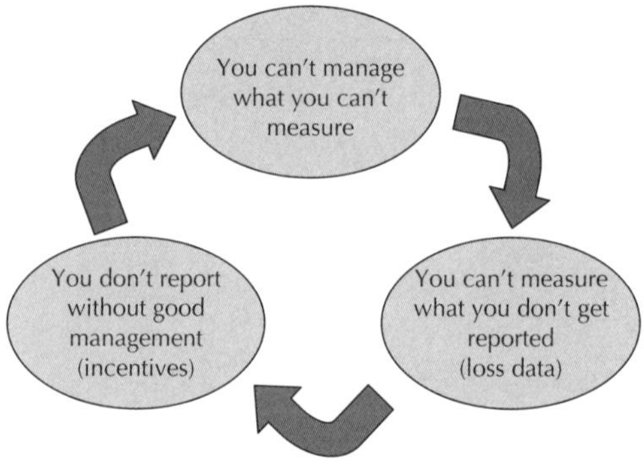

openness of the qualification criteria for AMA approaches, it is to be expected that, in future, further approaches will develop that cannot automatically and neatly be assigned to one of the three classes mentioned.

It should first be made clear that the quantification of operational risk, unlike the corresponding approaches in market and credit risk, is fundamentally dependent on subjective, ie, qualitative, elements. On the one hand, it is due to the special characteristic of this type of risk that it depends on processes, systems and employees specific to one bank; on the other hand, the inadequate availability of historical data is a contributory factor.

A much-cited saying in the risk management environment is, "You can't manage what you can't measure." Quite apart from the debate about how much truth is contained in this statement, it may be stressed that, in the area of operational risk, the thesis that says "You can't measure what you don't get reported" is valid. The basis of every existing model for quantification of operational risk is data that has either been collected and evaluated manually (eg, loss data) or reflects the opinion of experts (eg, scenarios). Again, incentives are required for complete and consistent collection, as already mentioned. "You don't report without good management."

Loss-distribution approaches are mostly based on actuarial models. A characteristic of actuarial approaches is the separate treatment and modelling of the frequency of loss events and the severity of their effects. This makes a more efficient exploitation of the data possible and also a more individual adjustment to changed circumstances (eg, an increase in frequency accompanied by an unchanged shape of the level distribution in the case of business expansion).

The objects of consideration are usually combinations of business lines and risk categories (eg, corporate clients/external events, called "cells"). This is due to the requirement that results should be obtained for individual business lines of the enterprise for management purposes, and that these usually differ from one to another in their risk profile. And on the other hand it is assumed that events in a risk category (usually event category) are homogeneous and thus conform to a common distribution. In principle, an individual distributional assumption in relation to the frequency and severity of losses could be made for each cell; however, in practice the poor availability of data mostly prevents full use being made of this option. In many cases one confines oneself to that choice of the same distribution class for all cells that can be empirically best supported.

As a rule, discrete distributions (count distributions) are used for modelling frequency. The classic (canonical) actuarial model is based on a Poisson distribution with the parameter λ, which simultaneously represents the mean and the standard deviation. Alternative forms of distribution are, for instance, the binomial distribution and the negative binomial distribution. The advantages of the Poisson distribution – also known as the distribution of rare events – include its robustness and its simple adjustment to altered data situations (eg, a change in the *de minimis* threshold).

Figure 39 Poisson distribution

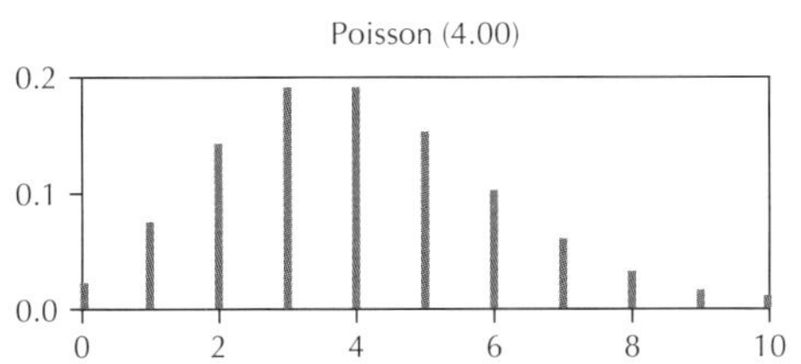

Figure 40 Lognormal distribution

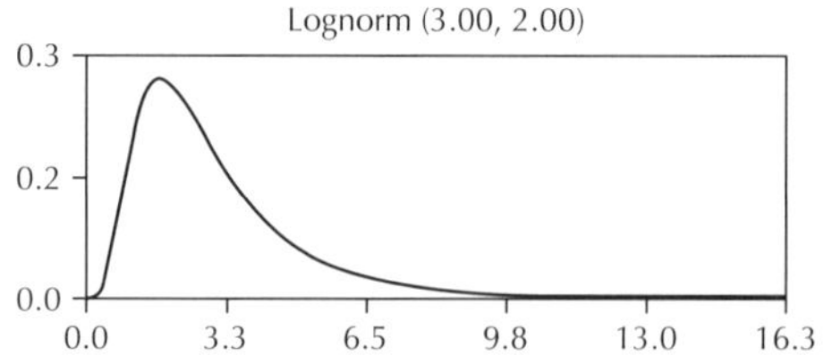

The severity of operational risk loss events is modelled using a continuous distribution. This must take the characteristics of the loss data into account. These include the asymmetry of the distribution and the fact that major losses occur with a distinctly higher probability than according to a corresponding normal distribution ("fat tail"). A large number of distributions are suitable here. Examples are the Pareto distribution, the lognormal distribution and the Weibull distribution. The eligible distributions have at least two parameters, which map location (mean μ) and dispersion (standard deviation σ). Moreover, some distributions also have a third parameter, which influences the shape (asymmetry) and in rare cases even a fourth parameter to control the kurtosis (fat tail). The choice of a severity distribution should, as in the case of the frequency distribution, take place on the basis of assumptions and, in view of the available data basis, in relation to the fit to the data.

A special case is the modelling focused on major losses (extreme value theory). This approach, which goes back to the late 19th century, was originally used to determine the required height of the dykes on the Dutch seacoast. It is not so much a question of the daily tidal range but more of the height of the spring tides. Thus, not the daily tide heights but the annual maximum of the tide heights were used as the data basis. For the modelling of operational risk one can similarly focus only on the biggest losses of a given period (block-maxima method) or on those losses that exceed a defined threshold (peaks-over-threshold method).

Parameter estimation methods must take into account the fact that the data to the left of a *de minimis* threshold is not available (truncation). They must further make a reliable derivation of the properties of the tail possible. The maximum likelihood estimation methods are fundamentally superior to the classic method of moment estimators, as they can be adjusted more flexibly to data situations.

With regard to the connection between frequency and severity, it is usually assumed that the distributions on which both are based are independent of each other – the loss count has no influence on the severity of the individual events. From the business point of view, this assumption appears to be often but not always justified.

In the example of the assumption of a Poisson distribution for the frequency of loss and a lognormal distribution for the severity of loss, the following representation of the total loss S ensues:

$$S = \sum_{i=0}^{N} L_i$$
$$N \sim \text{Po}(\lambda)$$
$$\ln L_i \sim \text{iid } N(\mu, \sigma)$$

Verbally, this means that the total loss S by a business line in one risk category corresponds to a stochastic sum of independent lognormally distributed individual losses L_i, whereby the number of summands follows a Poisson distribution.

Moreover, assumptions must be made regarding the correlations between events in different risk categories and/or business lines.

Figure 41 Steps of the modelling process

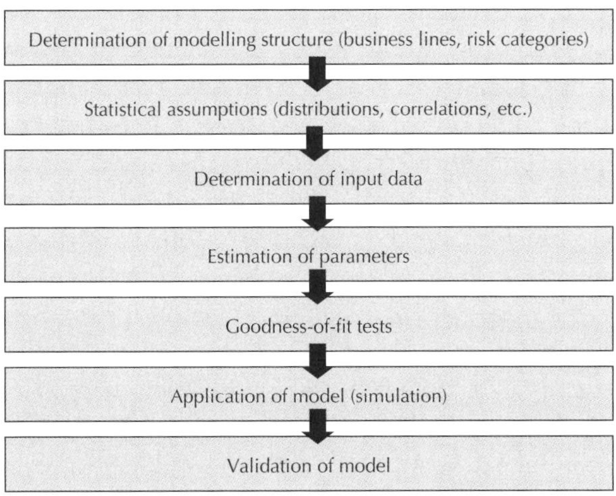

Since as a rule no adequate data basis is available to determine these empirically, determination must be made on the basis of expert opinions. Most frequently found is the assumption of zero correlation (correlation coefficient 0) or complete positive correlation (correlation coefficient 1).

An example of an uncorrelated pair of events would be "earthquake" and "internal criminal activities"; an example of a complete positive correlation is the breakdown of a central IT system that serves all business lines of the bank and thus leads to correlated events in different business lines. Convincing examples of negatively correlated events are seldom found in the area of operational risk.

An important point in the creation of a quantification model or the implementation of AMA models is the combination of knowledge obtained from different data sources (eg, internal loss data, data sharing data, external public data, scenario analysis).

A merger at the level of individual data is not advisable, as the data is collected in a completely different context and possesses specific distortions with regard to the frequency of observations in various areas of loss level (eg, due to varying *de minimis* thresholds during collection). In actuarial theory, credibility theory is employed for similar questions (joint use of internal and external data). This method assigns internal data more weight, as more internal information is available in relation to external information. A second possibility for the combination of different data sources is mixture distributions, which conceptually represents a generalisation of credibility theory.

Usually there is no closed-form solution for the combination of frequency and severity distributions. Thus, either approximation or simulation methods must be used. In the early days of actuarial theory, approximation methods were highly rated. However, the significance of approximation methods has decreased sharply in favour of simulation methods, because of the high performance of the computers usually available in banks and the increased flexibility embedded in simulation techniques.

For the performance of a Monte Carlo simulation, the model must be completely specified and parameterised. Each cell in a business line/event-category matrix is first of all treated separately. First a sample is taken from the corresponding frequency distribution. The result of the sampling determines the number of samples

Figure 42 Quantification results matrix

	People	Technology	...	Total
Private banking	VaR_{11}	VaR_{12}	VaR_{1j}	$VaR_{1\bullet}$
Investment banking	VaR_{21}	VaR_{22}	VaR_{2j}	$VaR_{2\bullet}$
...	VaR_{i1}	VaR_{i2}	VaR_{ij}	$VaR_{i\bullet}$
Whole bank				$VaR_{\bullet\bullet}$

from the severity distribution. The simulated individual losses are then added, and the procedure repeated very often (at least 100,000 times). Thus at the end of the simulation process a large number of possible loss realisations for the coming year are available.

The mean and the desired quantile are determined from such simulated results. In addition to the results obtained per cell, results of the marginal distributions, in particular with respect to business lines of the enterprise and the bank as a whole, taking a diversification effect into consideration could be calculated as well. Under the assumption of a lack of correlation between the business lines of the enterprise, the simulation results obtained for each risk category in the business line are summed without sorting and the desired quantile and mean are subsequently calculated.

As an alternative to various forms of the loss-distribution approach described above, several versions of the so-called scenario-based approach are under discussion. Under this approach, the parameters for the distribution of loss frequency and loss severity are not based on estimates from previous internal and external loss data, but rather on expert estimates within the framework of risk assessments or on the basis of scenario analysis. To some extent, external loss data is used as a starting point for the construction of scenarios; internal loss data usually serves to validate the models. Supporters of such a scenario-based approach cite the inadequate availability and/or the lack of validation of loss data as being the primary reason for this procedure.

The risk-drivers-and-controls approach is mostly based on a loss-distribution approach, the result of which is, however, more or less strongly modified by qualitative factors (usually gained within the framework of risk assessment or from KRIs). The qualitative elements are intended to extenuate the backward-looking nature of the loss data here as well.

A certain convergence of the various approaches is observable following the introduction of a requirements catalogue for the components of an advanced measurement approach (internal loss data, external data, scenario analysis, business environment and internal control factor). Nevertheless, it does not appear that a universally accepted procedure or a situation like in market risk (choice of a small number of best-practice methods, ie, variance–covariance approach, historical simulation or Monte Carlo simulation) will arise in the foreseeable future.

All models for the quantification of operational risk attempt to map the risk-mitigating effects of insurance. Insurance is an important instrument in active operational risk management. Of course it does not affect the frequency of losses or their actual financial consequences, but it affects the influence of such effects on the profit-and-loss account through partial or complete restitution for the damage suffered through compensation payments.

As the number and degree of cover for insurance policies concluded by the financial institution are not constant over time, modelling of loss severity distribution should, as described above, initially be based on the gross loss (ie, before deducting insurance payments). The current insurance cover can then be taken into account in the model as follows.

First, all currently existing insurance contracts must be mapped to the internal operational risk event categories. Since the insured risks are usually not identical with the event categories, a pragmatic assumption must be made concerning the degree of cover by insurance per risk category. This states what proportion of the losses incurred in a risk category can be expected to be covered by insurance.

An average deductible d (that part of the loss that the bank itself must bear) and an average coverage C (maximum insurance payment) must then be calculated for each risk category. These values can, depending on the specific provisions of the contract, relate either to the individual loss event or to the total loss per year (cumulative cover).

In the case of consideration by individual loss, the following relationship holds:

$$S = \sum_{i=0}^{N} X_i$$

$$X_i = \max(\tilde{X}_i - C + d, \min(\tilde{X}_i, d))$$

This means that the total loss S by a business line in one risk category corresponds to a stochastic sum of individual losses that have been reduced by the insurance cover paid.

The result of the quantification is thus an expected loss, which should be used in product pricing as a component of standard risk costs, and an unexpected loss (difference between quantile and expected value), which should be a component of the economic capital of the bank, together with the results from the other risk types. These values can be determined alternatively with and without taking the insurance payments into account, which supports an assessment of the advantageousness of existing insurance cover.

The use of the model as a basis of calculation of the regulatory capital requirement according to the AMA is subject to fulfilment of the supervisors' qualifying criteria, and the model must have received approval.

Model validation

An important step following the construction and application of the model is the validation in all dimensions (model input, model structure, model results and model implementation).

The first step is the validation of the model's input (in order to avoid interrelationships in the style of the saying "garbage in, garbage out"). It must first be checked whether all major influencing factors have been taken into account. In addition to examining how complete the internal and external data history is, this check includes the investigation of whether adjustments to the loss data – owing to altered type and level of business activities or because of systematic differences between the individual institution and the parties responsible for external losses – have been conducted in an adequate fashion. It must further be ensured that redundancies are avoided, eg, that one's own internal data are not included in the external data. The length of the data history is important up to the point where a limit of usability is reached because of the age of the information. Structural breaks owing to far-reaching alterations in processes, products and systems and possibly qualitative adjustments to the data must be taken into account.

Finally, the quality of the data is the single most important influencing factor of all. This includes, for example, the correct assignment to risk categories and business lines, the exactness of the loss amounts reported, the time of occurrence and so on. It should be borne in mind that distortions can occur, especially at the beginning of loss data collection, since the collection rate rises from a relatively low level and thus the number of losses reported, but not necessarily the number of losses incurred, rises. The scenarios used must be examined with regard to their quality and their cover of all important areas of operational risk. Similarly, the correct mapping of the business environment and internal control factor is important.

The majority of the potential problems relating to internal loss data can be successively remedied, at least in the course of time, by a suitably designed process of loss data collection and preparation that includes multilevel quality controls and comparisons with other sources of information (such as loss accounts). A bank usually has few possibilities of influencing the quality of external data, but consistency tests should nevertheless be carried out. Scenario analysis and business environment and internal control factors can to a certain extent be validated, eg by independent questioning of several experts.

The second step consists of the validation of the model with respect to its structure and fundamental assumptions. This involves examining how well the model is adjusted to reality, whereby it must be borne in mind that a model is always characterised by abstraction, idealisation and the reduction of complexity, and that thus a perfect fit to reality is impossible. The examination of the quality of the model can take place either with respect to partial aspects (such as the goodness of fit of the distribution for external criminal activities in the business line of corporate clients) or in its entirety (comparison of the suitability of two competing models).

Before using statistical methods, a check of plausibility and consistency should be carried out. For this purpose, the opinion of experts not involved in the construction of the model can be obtained, who are able to examine the model for its logical consistency and discover facts that contradict intuition and experience.

A number of methods for examining the goodness of fit of the distribution are available. These include statistical tests (t-test, χ^2-test, rank correlations) and graphic methods (histograms, QQ plots). Particular relevance should be assigned to the quality of fit of higher moments (skewness, kurtosis) and the tail of the distribution. On the other hand, an overfitting (the use of too many parameters and the false impression of an increase in the accuracy of the fit) is to be avoided, as the sensitivity of the model to only slightly changed data tends to rise with an increase in the complexity of the model. The smaller the available data basis is, the more graphic methods should come to the forefront, since the expressiveness of statistical tests is generally too limited.

When examining the overall quality of the model, the key question is how probable it is that the input data would have been generated by the model used. In the case of the employment of maximum likelihood estimation methods, likelihood ratio tests can be used to assess the quality of the adjustment. Alternatively, the selection of the model can be undertaken with the help of information criteria – Akaike Information Criterion (AIC) or Bayes Information Criterion (BIC). These methods take into account the fact that, other things being equal, a model with a higher number of degrees of freedom (a higher number of parameters) permits a better adjustment to the data basis. Therefore, the number of parameters used in the model is taken into account with a penalty function.

Lastly, the model's output must be validated. This usually consists of expected values and high quantiles (eg, 99.9%) of the loss distribution. The validation of quantiles naturally causes the biggest problems, but even the verification of the expected value itself is not easy, as this is influenced by rare, high losses, while these are not, or are insufficiently, present in reference histories.

The backtesting procedure is known in the area of market risk. The method compares forecast portfolio value changes with actual fluctuations in value (profit and loss). Given a holding period customary for market risk of one day and a confidence level of 99%, this means that, on average (assuming 250 trading days a year), the

VaR will be exceeded 2.5 times a year. It is then possible using statistical methods to verify whether the actual number of overruns significantly deviates from the expected value.

On the basis of the usual holding period for operational risk of one year and the confidence level of at least 99.9% selected for regulatory or economic capital management reasons, a direct transfer of the method is excluded: an overrun would be expected on average once in 1,000 years, which, on this basis, makes model output validation carried out a minimum of once a year impossible.

A further method of verifying the quality of the model – also known in the area of market risk – is stress testing. This examines the extent to which the model is in a position to map extreme constellations and leads to correct forecasts within a defined tolerance. Owing to the different nature of the data basis in respect of operational risk, the analogous implementation of such methods is impossible; however, an attempt can be made to conduct appropriate investigations with scenario analysis.

The necessity of calibration of the model can result from the verification of the quality of the model. This means that model parameters that cannot be derived from objective data are adjusted such that the output of the model moves within a range consistent with reality. This tuning of the model, which is also common in physics, may however be undertaken only in a plausible manner. In particular, care must be taken that, during the repeated use of the model over time, no arbitrary adjustments of the calibration values originally undertaken become necessary that cannot be explained on the basis of substantially altered underlying conditions.

Lastly, it is necessary to examine the extent to which the technical IT implementation of the quantification model was carried out correctly. This includes, on the one hand, an examination of the extent to which mathematical formulas were converted to corresponding programme code. On the other hand it is necessary to ensure that the algorithms used in the programme meet the requirements. In particular, the quality of the random-number generator and its transformation to the chosen distributional assumption is decisive. Frequent inadequacies of the relevant software modules are clusters of random numbers in certain regions, correlations within the random-number series and numerical problems (eg, the ability to distinguish between numbers close to zero and zero itself).

Economic capital

Economic capital (risk capital) is the capital that individual business lines of a bank need in order to cushion the risks from their business operations with a predetermined probability. The probability that the economic capital will not be sufficient to do so is usually equated with the target rating (and thus with the target probability of default) of the institution.

The risk capital assigned to the individual business lines is usually linked to a target interest rate (hurdle rate). Thus the profitability of each business line can be uniformly assessed taking the revenues, costs and risks into account (risk-adjusted performance measurement).

Operational risk must be taken into account when determining the economic capital that relates to the overall risk content of the bank. Models oriented to the requirements of AMAs are basically suitable for depicting a contribution to economic capital. By contrast, the use of the results of the basic-indicator or standardised approach for such purposes is problematic, since the inadequate risk sensitivity of such methods can lead to wrong management decisions.

When determining economic capital, differing confidence levels and holding periods for the various risk components should possibly be taken into consideration. Moreover, the correlation among the various risk types plays an important role. While in the unrealistic case of complete correlation the results from the various risk types can be added, significantly lower capital amounts result from incomplete correlation or indeed from zero correlation. The determination of these, which can be based to some extent on copulas, as in the case of capital models for operational risk, will not be further elaborated on here, because of its very technical nature.

RISK INFORMATION TECHNOLOGY

Risk IT denotes the IT infrastructure needed to support the process of operational risk management. This can range from simple, Microsoft Office-based data-entry forms for the collection of loss data and the performance of risk assessments up to specialised integrated, web-based applications and databases.

The requirements on IT support are essentially determined by the size and complexity of the financial institution (number of branches, foreign subsidiaries and so forth) and also the technical requirements. A secondary constraint should be the minimisation of central administrative effort required, in view of the staff capacities usually available. The number of integrated systems available has increased significantly in recent years, although no market leader has yet succeeded in establishing itself. Some software packages have been developed within the framework of corresponding commissions by individual banks and subsequently provided with increased flexibility to cover the wishes of a broader customer base; others were conceived from the outset as standard software and offered in the marketplace. All have in common that, because of the lack of standardisation, certain methodological or process-related decisions always had to be made in developing them, which for the individual user frequently entail a commitment to particular methods or procedures.

Fundamental demands on an IT system

Basic functions of integrated software packages for operational risk are decentralised data entry (loss data, risk indicators, replies to risk assessment questionnaires), decentralised *ad hoc* evaluation in the various business lines (evaluation of loss data histories, computation of business line-specific indicator scores, determination of a risk assessment rating), centralised evaluation across all business lines (determination of regulatory and economic capital, aggregation and comparative presentation of the results of all components of operational risk for board reporting purposes) and centralised and/or decentralised administration (user data and other static data).

The choice of a particular software product should always be oriented towards the functional and technical requirements and not, conversely, the design of the methods of managing and controlling operational risk restricted to the available functionality of the tool selected.

Table 10 Examples of requirements on an IT system

Content-related	Technical
Data-archiving methods	Databases supported
Data-import functions	Programming language used
Data-export functions	Encryption method
Workflow support	Multi-user concept
Reporting functions	Multi-firm capability
Extendibility of data fields	Performance
Graphic displays	Hardware requirements
User roles and rights	Operating system requirements
User-friendliness	Requirements for additional software
Customisability	Implementation period

If so desired, interfaces with other systems (eg, the automatic capture of risk indicators) must exist; the basis of decision here should be a cost–benefit analysis, in view of the low capture frequency in many cases.

Specifically to ensure usability for AMA models, the main demand on an IT system is the accumulation of consistent data histories. These include internal and external loss data, detailed results and also ratings from risk assessments and risk indicators, as well as evaluations based thereon (economic and regulatory capital).

The main difficulty with archiving data relating to operational risk consists particularly in restructurings and the reclassification of data occurrences resulting from them. This demonstrates once more the importance of a uniform data structure for all components. It must moreover be ensured that changes to the data histories based on new knowledge or supplementary information are possible (eg, in the case of subsequent loss mitigation due to insurance refunds).

A further important aspect is the IT and internal audit security of the system. On the one hand it must be ensured that stored confidential data is accessible only by authorised persons. Thus, protection against unauthorised access from both inside and outside the bank is necessary. On the other hand, in particular the data used for the computation of regulatory and economic capital must be protected against manipulation.

Furthermore, the derivation of results relevant to management and also those prescribed for supervisory purposes must be transparent at all times. From this results the necessity of a discriminating policy for access rights among users – eg, in the style of an internal multi-firm capability (per business line/department).

Thus, it would be possible to grant local read/write rights to decentralised operational risk managers for the creation and release of data records, local read-only rights to decentralised line management for *ad hoc* reporting purposes and global read/write rights to operational risk control for the adjustment of data and for global reporting. Global read-only rights could be granted to internal audit for evaluation purposes and administrator rights to operational risk control for the creation and modification of users, structure, etc.

The ability to reconstruct all data must be guaranteed by an appropriate database concept and audit trails (recording all transactions in the system). Backup concepts must hinder data loss because of technical failures.

The IT system should support the relevant workflow of the operational risk management process (capture, modification, release, deactivation and so on) and thus ensure that all necessary process steps are carried out and consequently no unconfirmed data is drawn on for evaluation purposes. A practical workflow combined with ergonomic criteria is furthermore an effective measure to ensure – as far as possible – a complete and consistent data collection, since possible inhibition thresholds for the effective use of the system are slight. The user-friendliness of the system must also be seen in this connection, which should keep the hurdles for the use of the software as low as possible.

Implementation of operational risk management methods

IT support for the operational risk management methods described above is always subject to specific requirements. The subsystem for the capture of loss data should ideally consist of a web-based, decentralised data-entry tool, an automated authorisation procedure depending on the loss level, control mechanisms for the avoidance of double entries and also the possibility of centralised evaluation and aggregation by risk control and internal audit, as needed. A procedure for adjusting historical losses to changes in the structure of the bank – eg, in the case of organisational changes – is also very convenient. Since a large number of employees with different levels of experience, in particular in categorising and the exact determination of the level of loss, are involved in entering the loss data, a comprehensive (online) help system is essential here.

Insofar as external loss data is purchased, an interface with the data format of the supplier is needed, or at least the facility to upload larger quantities of data. Since the data format may change during the course of time, a great degree of flexibility in this respect is advisable. A control mechanism for avoiding double entries in the course of the updates that take place on a regular basis is also useful. The implementation of assignment rules, eg, from internal categories to Basel categories in the form of mapping tables, permits the adjustment of the internal bank structure to external requirements.

In order to participate in data-sharing initiatives, an export mechanism for internal loss data must be created, with corresponding mapping rules from the internal structure to the common structure, analogously to the import mechanism. Ideally, the standardisation and the rendering anonymous of the data would also be supported.

A further function worth mentioning in the area of loss data is the centralised or decentralised creation and modification of scenarios in the sense of fictitious data.

In the case of IT support for risk assessment, the emphasis is on the decentralised processing of questionnaires, checklists and risk matrices that are maintained centrally, and, if possible, support for workshops to be conducted for the purpose of deriving results. A workflow should ensure that the dual-control principle is observed. In order to simplify the intensive use of the system, in particular also for decentralised risk management, a large degree of decentralised functions should be present in addition to centralised possibilities for evaluation. Otherwise the acceptance needed to ensure use in all business lines of the bank will be hampered. Comparisons between several periods and across different units of the bank are a further indispensable component.

Software functions for managing risk indicators permit the centralised or decentralised definition of risk indicators as well as the decentralised and regular entry of the relevant risk indicator values, in individual cases by means of direct links with a corresponding supplier system. Plausibility checking of entries is useful; the manner of handling missing data must be specified. Depending on the concept adopted, multilevel threshold values must be definable centrally or decentrally; multilevel aggregation logic with special rules for the avoidance of undesired levelling effects is required. As early-warning systems based on risk indicators are used by some banks as central instruments for managing operational risk, it is of special importance here to adjust the functionality to the requirements of day-to-day business. The inclusion of measure tracking can represent a meaningful addition to a risk-indicator system.

A computational engine for regulatory and economic capital brings all data from the above-named components together, depending on the concept employed. Of importance here is the possibility for internal audit to reconstruct the results determined, since these are used directly for external (supervisory) reporting and for managing the bank. The individual data sources must be freely selectable at the technical level (by means of appropriate filters and similar interfaces). It must be possible for the user to define distribution assumptions for each risk category and business line, including dependency structures and settings for the calculation (desired quantile, number of iterations).

A management information system brings together all available information appropriate to each addressee. This makes possible the derivation of measures from the comparison of results from various instruments (eg, loss data collection and risk indicators), over several periods (eg, quarterly comparisons) as well as across all business lines of the bank. The management information system should support both the preparation of regular reports in a standardised format and flexible *ad hoc* evaluation on the computer screen. Whether this takes place in traditional paper form or electronically is at the discretion of the user, but a print function should at least be available.

6

Implementation of the Framework Components and Management Process

The implementation of a complete framework for operational risk management is dependent on many aspects, most of them specific to the institution concerned. Material in this case are:

- preliminary conditions:
  - organisational structure and complexity of the financial institution;
  - pre-existing risk management process elements and risk culture;
  - existing IT environment;
- objectives:
  - implementation approaches selected (Basel Approaches or desired good or best practice standards);
  - planned implementation period, possibly phased plan;
- resources:
  - human resources;
  - budget;
  - availability of external resources.

External aspects such as the behaviour of competitors, specific industry standards and the expectations of the national banking supervisors and those of other countries – in the event of international activities – all play a role. They also require careful management, but they are of subordinate significance for the concrete implementation.

APPROACH

In spite of all potential differences with regard to preliminary conditions, objectives and planned commitment of resources between individual banks, there is fundamentally a far-reaching general approach. Since operational risk cannot be restricted to a few areas of a bank – from which it follows that the management framework must embrace all areas at the latest in the final stage – the approach represents to a large extent a fundamental process reorganisation. Independently of the size and complexity of the institution, a four-phase approach suggests itself:

- Phase 1: the analysis of the current position and the planning of the target position;
- Phase 2: design and implementation of the framework;
- Phase 3: trial phase (use test) and adjustment; and
- Phase 4: day-to-day operation and continuing development.

Phase 1: The analysis of the current position and the planning of the target position

Phase 1 consists of a fundamental definition of the position. First, all relevant requirements for a management framework and the components necessary for this are laid down. Ideally, this should take the shape of a documented requirements catalogue. In the course of all this, the requirements can be separated into internal and external ones.

Internal requirements

The fulfilment of internal requirements on the entire framework for the management and controlling of operational risk is mainly marked by several things:

- a market position either in existence or aspired to – the market leader will fundamentally be more inclined to implement current best-practice methods and procedures, in particular dependent on:
  - the quality of risk management as a whole;
  - the risk content of major activities, markets and products; and
  - the decision for or against the management of economic capital;
- the expectation, by means of consistent management structures and processes for reducing the risks and costs of a type of risk ie,

considered to be, after credit risk, the biggest for a bank, and to obtain a competitive advantage, thereby:

  - ❑ optimising the insurance programme;
  - ❑ improved outsourcing controlling; and
  - ❑ the reduction of risks and losses in the value chain;

- ❑ apparently slightly paradoxically, expectations determined from outside, formed by rating agencies and counterparties, which, although fundamentally not defining any internal requirements, reveal that certain standards are expected, or that sanctions will be incurred if they are not reached – ie, to say:

  - ❑ rating agencies;
  - ❑ counterparties; and
  - ❑ customers.

These three drivers are by no means independent. A market leader will be generally prepared to invest in the most progressive methods, which is always more costly than for the imitators. Following successful implementation, corresponding advantages arise from this, eg through optimising the insurance programme, an improved outsourcing controlling or simply an improvement in the quality of core processes. Correspondingly, the expectations of third parties are not independent of self-image and postulated objectives. The aspect of standard setting should not be overlooked. Owing to the continuing extensive discussion concerning all aspects of organisational structure and process design, active influence can be exerted on such discussion.

Depending on the objectives set, the internal requirements – differentiated by business line or subsidiary if so desired – must be defined accordingly.

External demands

Because of the current regulatory discussion it is expedient to define at least the regulatory requirements depending on all three permissible approaches (basic indicators, standardised approach and AMAs). In view of the size and complexity of the bank, there may already be some idea on the part of the banking supervision as to which minimum approach will need to be fulfilled. Independently of this, the requirements of all three approaches should be included in the evaluation, since basically the option may exist to pursue different approaches (partial use) in different organisational units, at least for a limited period of time.

The actual or aimed-for market position or market perception will have just as much influence on the extent and quality as the regulatory constraints. A market leader will be at pains to implement or indeed to define and continuously develop best practice, however vague that concept might be. Banks in the midfield of their market will tend to define lower internal demands, while small banks traditionally first implement minimum requirements before further-reaching elements are evaluated.

Requirements catalogue

Considerable room for interpretation exists both in the Basel requirements and in those requirements needing to be formulated internally. This can be taken advantage of, but also holds the risk of not working or not being, or being insufficiently, fulfilled under subsequent external verification. With regard to external appraisers, banking supervision, external auditors, rating agencies and business partners, constant, purposeful communication is beneficial. At the moment, the same uncertainty is present for all involved, but not the same risk in the event of misinterpretation. It is therefore essential to discuss and review your own ideas regularly with the relevant counterparty. Everyone agrees at present that neither the development nor the learning process is complete, and includes themselves explicitly. There are also differences of opinion between the banking supervisory authorities of the various countries, which are reflected in the extension of the parallel-run phase for the AMA for operational risk and for the most advanced credit risk approach. Corresponding management of the expectations of third parties involved is therefore a necessary element of the implementation of a framework for operational risk.

Analysis of current position

The analysis of the current position follows on the definition of the relevant requirements. In this, all areas that were historically entrusted with aspects of operational risk management should in any event be included. A limitation to those who are intended to play a role in the future framework is short-sighted. These include, in addition to the existing risk management and risk-controlling units in all areas of the bank or group, such areas as IT (especially IT security, emergency planning), insurance, human resources, legal, money laundering, and compliance. In many cases, internal audit has in the past undertaken risk management and risk-controlling tasks and hence should be included. Frequently, methods or processes that can be used as further components of the future framework are to be found in individual areas. Thus the use of indicators in back-office areas is frequently current practice, and loss data are collected in connection with quality management initiatives or by internal audit. In many cases risk assessments already exist in various forms. Subsidiaries have also often undertaken significant efforts independently of the parent, which can be of use to the entire group.

In the most favourable case, existing components can be retained and transferred, with minor adjustments, to the entire bank. However, experience shows that this is seldom the case, since they were often conceived for a limited, specific area. More frequently, components are found that can be seen as a proof of concept and offer a basis for further development. The advantage in their use over a new development is that they have already been introduced and correspondingly less resistance to further development is experienced than in the case of a completely new methodology. For example, in many cases a loss data collection process may be found. Even though neither the extent nor the organisational cover of that particular process may fulfil the formulated requirements, it can serve as evidence that the condition aspired to is far less new and revolutionary than sceptics claim.

Derivation of the gaps

The determination of the gaps follows the analysis of the current position. The more systematically the requirements were defined, the simpler this step is. It is obvious, therefore, that the gaps will vary depending on the approach selected or the understanding of best practice. It generally makes sense to conduct an analysis of the gaps and evaluate them against all other options, even if they are intuitively not considered to be relevant. Only in this way can real alternative courses of action be determined in the subsequent analysis of effects. A predetermination is not advisable, in view of the relatively minor effort of analysis, and, depending on the result, originally unplanned alternatives can become eligible as alternative courses of action.

Effects and cost–benefit analyses

The analysis of effects undertakes a cost–benefit consideration of alternative courses of action and the associated costs of conception and implementation. In the course of this, it will be necessary to work with considerable assumptions and with uncertainty, in particular in the case of weighing the benefits. While the effects on the regulatory capital under Pillar 1 for the basic indicator and standardised approaches can easily be determined, this is virtually impossible for an AMA, since this methodology will already be implemented in only the fewest cases. Moreover, uncertainty as to how national supervisors will make use of their freedom under Pillar 2 prevails for all approaches. While Anglo-Saxon countries already have experience with this, the concept of qualitative supervision is rather new in Continental Europe. In order to be able nevertheless to conduct an appropriate analysis, the "best case" – namely that a reduction of regulatory capital down to the permitted floor (including credit risk) will be possible – should be assumed for the potential benefit of an AMA. For a bank it seems unlikely that the use of such a quantification method would otherwise be aspired to. Should a higher value be determined than under the standardised approach, it would be irrational not to use the more favourable approach.

If possible, one would wait with the official announcement of the development of AMAs until the models are more stable and the risk factors influencing them can be better managed. Cost–benefit considerations with regard to best practice are still considerably more uncertain, since up to now no well-founded statements can be made about the monetary benefit of good or better operational risk management, because of quantification problems. There is indeed a consensus that there is a link between clear assignment of tasks and responsibilities, complete loss data collection, a comprehensive risk assessment programme and an overall lower operational risk, but the level is not quantifiable. In this connection it is often forgotten that also investment in market and credit risk management does not lead in the first place to a reduction of risk, but to better measurement of the same and also to improved management instruments. The decision on a reduction of these risks is a downstream step on the basis of extended information and an improved range of instruments.

The cost side can today be comparatively easily evaluated on the basis of available experience. If, due to the absence of prior projects within the bank or group little knowledge is present concerning the necessary costs, the expenses can also be determined with the help of external support.

Planning implementation

Based on this cost–benefit analysis, the bank's board of directors can make a decision on the components to be implemented, their extent and their chronological order. Experience shows that this analysis is carried out in several iterative steps, so as to bring the situation aspired to closer to the available means committed. Even taking the compulsory regulatory requirements into account, an AMA can initially be implemented only in selected pilot business lines, by way of partial use, before this is then rolled out to the entire bank or bank group, for reasons of cost or capacity. Within this framework, the last step is corresponding detailed planning of all necessary components, tasks, resources and the chronological order.

Phase 2: Design and implementation of the framework

Depending on the elements planned in Phase 1, the design and (pilot) implementation of all components follows in Phase 2. Even though in theory and in practice many components are closely interrelated or are built directly on one other, a parallel development of the complete framework will be undertaken in only the fewest cases. For one thing, a lack of capacity often prevents this; for another some components require considerable time both in their development and in their implementation. The design of the various methods takes place in the draft stage. Furthermore, at first only a pilot implementation or a simple implementation can be carried out for some of the components, which can then be improved during the course of the project, as required. However, not all elements lend themselves to the same extent to both or one of these steps.

Table 11 Prerequisites for the implementation of framework components

Framework component	Dependence on	Elements	Prerequisite for	Timing of implementation
Risk strategy	Overall risk strategy of the bank, especially scope regarding market, credit and other risks	Intentional alignment of the results by means of discussions	All subsequent framework components	Due to the fundamental character prerequisite for all subsequent framework components; depending on the implementation plan modifications and enhancements possible
Framework	Overall risk management structure of the bank as well as the overall organisation	Roles and responsibilities of all involved parties, that is to say, board of directors, business unit heads, department heads, risk control and internal audit	All subsequent framework components	Due to the fundamental character prerequisite for all subsequent framework components; depending on the implementation plan modifications and enhancements possible
Definitions and structures	Risk strategy and framework	Definition of operational risk; risk categories on different levels; definition of business line/event type mapping; organisational structure	All subsequent framework components	Component to be implemented first, possibly in parallel with risk strategy and framework

Loss data	Definitions and structures, risk strategy and framework	Definition and components of internal and external loss data; data gathering process; roles and responsibilities	Quantification and reporting	Full implementation from the start advisable; test in a sufficiently large pilot area possible
Risk assessment	Definitions and structures, risk strategy and framework	Subjects of evaluation; evaluation methodology and process	Reporting	Full implementation from the start advisable; test in a sufficiently large pilot area possible
Key risk indicators	Definitions and structures, risk strategy and framework	Definition; process of data gathering; thresholds; aggregation techniques	Reporting	Full implementation from the start advisable; test in a sufficiently large pilot area possible
Management information system	All elements mentioned above	Roles and responsibilities; goals; reporting process; IT implementation	Continuous management of operational risk	Stepwise with the introduction of individual elements
Economic and regulatory capital	All elements mentioned above, depending on the chosen methodology	Model used in practice; parameter; process; validation; usage in bank steering	Regulatory reporting; bank steering through economic capital	Stepwise model development depending on availability of input parameters
Risk IT	Requirements catalogue of the element to cover	Requirements on hardware and software; support of other components; IT governance and maintenance	Management and reporting	Stepwise implementation depending on the technical requirements of other elements

Since the various components of the framework for operational risk management have different premises, they can to some extent be conceived and implemented only sequentially. The extent to which a possible parallel development and implementation should be carried out depends – apart from the interdependencies described above – essentially on the available capacities.

Phase 3: Trial phase (use test) and adjustment

The components implemented are subject to a final test in the trial and adjustment phase. This phase should be communicated as such to all concerned. Even given existing experience, it cannot be guaranteed that errors might be made in the prior phases that come to light only during trials. Not infrequently, procedures that are deemed to be tried do not operate in the manner expected, because of certain organisational peculiarities of the institution concerned. This possibility should be known to all involved, so that the necessary trial and possible adjustment phase does not appear to be an unplanned phase of error correction but rather an expected step that was planned as such. The covering up of errors so as to counter a possibly negative impression is understandable but mistaken. However, if it turns out that the necessary alterations go beyond adjustments, it can make sense to relegate the components concerned to the draft phase. Planning was possibly conducted under false assumptions or mistakes have been made in the implementation.

Phase 4: Day-to-day operation and continuing development

Following a successful use test of individual or all components, the framework moves into the day-to-day operation phase. For some components this can be the final state of construction, but for many it will be a phase of bank-wide use with increasing intensity. Owing to the necessity of internal adjustments and further external development, all components of the framework will in the course of time have to be reviewed and possibly adjusted on a regular basis.

MANPOWER AND TIME INVOLVED

The manpower and time involved in implementing an operational risk management framework is dependent to a large extent on the tasks needed in the various phases. They are spread over a large number of business lines and possibly include external consultants. Depending on the organisational positioning of the project, the main emphasis of the project work will lie in the area of risk control and move specifically – if present – to the area of operational risk control. Because of the relevance of the project for the entire bank, nearly all areas will be involved during the course of the project, at least in the short term. Should a bank decide in favour of an implementation procedure with one or more pilot business lines, these will correspondingly be under more pressure. Fundamentally, the pressure on manpower and time can be managed by the deployment of more or fewer external resources, whereby in the final analysis the corresponding relief is replaced by greater financial expense. But it should be borne in mind here that this makes sense only to a certain extent. Thus essential conceptional work and experience in the implementation of these concepts can be supplied by external providers. However, the participation of the largest possible number of internal resources is advisable, in particular in the development of components such as definitions and structures, the questions and procedures for risk assessment and the determination of risk indicators. The external view can never exhibit the necessary specific detailed knowledge, and the necessary acceptance of the processes and methods to be implemented can be ensured only by the intensive involvement of the bank's own employees.

Because it is difficult, owing to specific requirements and individual preliminary conditions, to present a generic and complete project for the implementation of a framework for the management and control of operational risk, two alternative project plans are to be found below, one of them oriented towards best practice and towards implementation of AMAs in a large bank, and one towards the implementation of average marketplace standards with conformity to the standardised approach. Obviously, both are to be understood only as approximate orientation assistance. The individual preliminary conditions can be very different in all cases. If, for example, a comprehensive loss data collection process or a risk assessment programme has been in existence for a long time, considerable time savings can be realised. Precisely these two areas require considerable time for their implementation, because of the extensive learning and training process.

Figure 43 A best practice/AMA-oriented implementation project

ID	Task Name	Duration
1	**Current analysis**	**60 days**
5	**Design and implementation**	**660 days**
6	Risikostrategie	5 days
7	**Framework**	**540 days**
8	Design	180 days
9	Implementation	360 days
10	**Definitions & structures**	**90 days**
11	Design	60 days
12	Implementation	30 days
13	**Loss data**	**390 days**
14	Design	30 days
15	Implementation	360 days
16	**Risk assessment**	**240 days**
17	Design	60 days
18	Implementation	180 days
19	**Key risk indicators**	**240 days**
20	Design	60 days
21	Implementation	180 days
22	**Management Information System**	**120 days**
23	Design	30 days
24	Implementation	90 days
25	**Economic and regulatory capital**	**123 days**
26	Design	30 days
27	Implementation	60 days
28	**Risk IT**	**80 days**
29	Design	40 days
30	Implementation	40 days
31	**Testing**	**90 days**
32	**Day-to-day business**	**0 day**

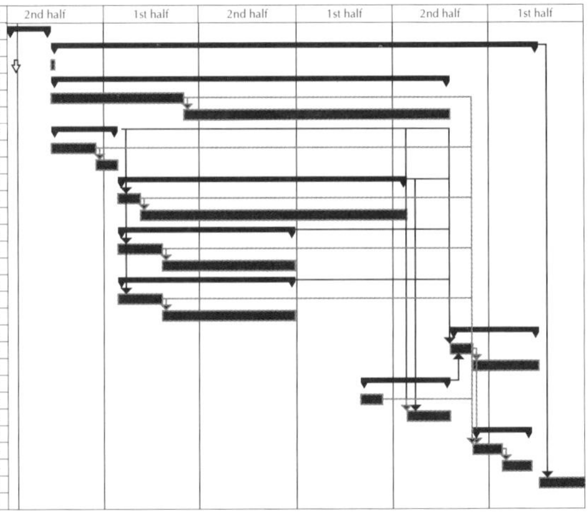

Figure 44 A good practice/TSA-oriented implementation project

ID	Task Name	Duration
1	**Current analysis**	**60 days**
5	**Design and implementation**	**262 days**
6	Risikostrategie	5 days
7	**Framework**	**150 days**
8	Design	60 days
9	Implementation	90 days
10	**Definitions & structures**	**60 days**
11	Design	30 days
12	Implementation	30 days
13	**Loss data**	**110 days**
14	Design	20 days
15	Implementation	90 days
16	**Risk assessment**	**110 days**
17	Design	20 days
18	Implementation	90 days
19	**Key risk indicators**	**110 days**
20	Design	20 days
21	Implementation	90 days
22	**Management Information System**	**60 days**
23	Design	20 days
24	Implementation	40 days
25	**Regulatory capital**	**45 days**
26	Design	15 days
27	Implementation	30 days
28	**Risk IT**	**40 days**
29	Design	20 days
30	Implementation	20 days
31	**Testing**	**45 days**
32	**Day-to-day business**	**0 day**

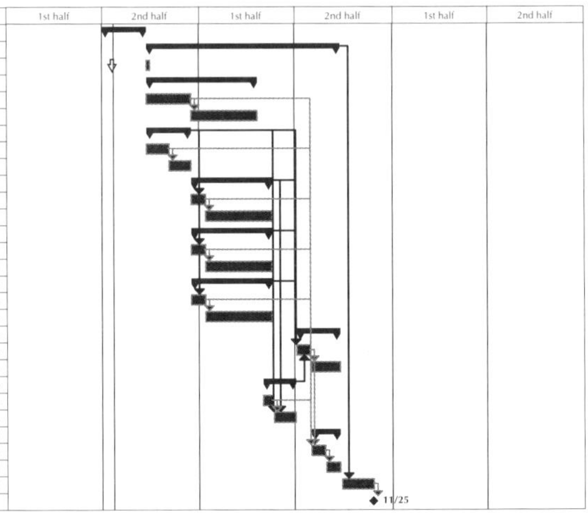

A different distribution of the effort is possible to a certain extent. In particular, the components framework, risk assessment and risk indicators can be stretched out more. However, it should be borne in mind that there are certain interdependencies. It is thus not necessary to implement a complete management structure as early as the first half of the project. Owing to the absence of instruments and management information, it would not be possible for this structure to function adequately. On the other hand, a minimum amount should be implemented early on, so as to obtain suitable contact persons with clear responsibilities, eg for data collection. The effort required for risk indicator and risk assessment is especially marked by the significant involvement of the specialised areas and mostly of the same persons. If this cannot be guaranteed, the two components should not be implemented simultaneously.

IMPLEMENTATION PROBLEMS

Projects for the implementation of a framework for operational risk management are not really capable of failing, because of the regulatory requirements and the large number of components to be implemented. However, considerably less benefit may be derived from the components in the event of a defective implementation, or a less advanced regulatory approach may be implemented than originally planned. The question of whether this will have consequences on the part of the banking supervisors cannot at present be answered, because of the lack of experience with the implementation of the Basel Pillar 2. Neither case is desirable, representing a misallocation of resources as they always do. There are several major success factors for the correct implementation, such as support from the board, an appropriate corporate culture, clearly defined project aims and adequate resources in terms of staff and finance.

Owing to the far-reaching nature of an implementation project for operational risk management, the factors named – and, if relevant, further bank-specific factors – should be analysed beforehand. There is, indeed, little temporal latitude for the implementation of the regulatory requirements, but, on the whole, the question of whether the intended implementation period is promising should be critically examined. If the bank is currently carrying out other

Table 12 Success factors of an implementation project

Success factor	Risk	Effect	Measures
Board support	Missing support by the management board; the project is seen just as a regulatory necessity, not as a means of improving risk management	Lacking power of the project management; weak management of operational risk	Ongoing communication; identification of a board member as a sponsor; quick wins
Corporate culture	Weak corporate culture or strong control culture that does not serve business goals	Risk management will be seen as a must; controls as an end in themselves but not as a means of supporting the business	Ongoing communication; board support; quick wins for all parties involved
Responsibilities	Unclear responsibilities in both the project and the risk management organisation	Ineffective management due to unclear responsibilities; delay in decision making; unclear escalation channels	Definition of a clear project structure; willingness at board level to establish a strong management structure linked to the organisation
Risk definition	Unclear boundaries between risk types	Management responsibilities in areas of overlap unclear; low data quality; erroneous management information	Clear definition of all risk types as a prerequisite for an operational risk project
Limited focus on quantification	Too strong focus on quantification	Overemphasis of currently unstable quantification methods; lacking importance of	Ongoing communication of the early stage of

		necessary process changes; lack of credibility	development of quantification methods; focus on changes to organisation and processes
Integrated risk reporting	Establishment of a parallel MIS inconsistent to existing management reporting	Unclear flow of information; inferior basis for management decisions; duplication of efforts for senders and receivers	Integration of risk reporting in existing MIS at an early stage
Qualified resources	Insufficient availability of resources	Delayed or suboptimal implementation	Realistic planning; Buy-in by responsible parties
Project management	Weak project management	Insufficient or delayed project execution; breach of budget and deadlines; lacking acceptance of the management framework	Experienced project management; clear deliverables and escalation channels; adequate resources; realistic goals
Training	Lacking or inadequate training	Ineffective implementation of the management components; insufficient use; poor data quality	Design and implementation of trainings as integral part of the implementation project

projects with a high priority – eg, the conversion to International Financial Reporting Standards (IFRS) or the implementation of fundamentally new IT systems – the burden on resources can become too great, in particular in the business lines of the bank. In this case, close consultation with the existing projects is necessary. It may be possible to make use of synergies. For instance, the construction of a new database for credit risk management and for accounting according to IFRS could be taken as an opportunity to examine relevant cases as to their operational risk components.

It is not very beneficial to begin a comprehensive project with ambitious aims and then not to carry it through as planned. As a rule, business lines can be convinced of extensive changes on only a few occasions. A repeated attempt, for example, to create a loss data collection process will likely be interpreted as a fundamental flaw in the approach. Experience shows that the necessary support will be lower on repeated attempts.

If these risks to a planned project are present, it can make sense, in the absence of board support, to focus, as a first step, on the regulatory (minimum) requirements, or to concentrate on a few pilot business lines. At the same time, the expected benefit for all decision makers should be presented in a process of permanent communication. If there are projects competing for resources, close consultation with the appropriate persons responsible for the projects can in many cases identify those excess resource capacities that are necessary for successful implementation.

An essential feature of good project management remains the management of the expectations of all involved. In a project planned for a period of two to three years in a dynamic environment in which further refinement of the methods is not only expected but explicitly desired by all participants, departures from the original project plan are likely. In such cases, clear communication of the reasons and consequences is essential, in order to receive the necessary acceptance and support over the entire life of the project.

7
Outlook

The consistent implementation of a comprehensive range of instruments for the management and control of operational risk leads to significant changes in the day-to-day and – if not directly then at least in the medium term – strategic business of a bank. Current discussion shows that the content-oriented – in particular the quantitative and IT – dimension tends to be overestimated, while the organisational and qualitative dimension tends to be underestimated. The latter plays an important role in view of the significance for the entire bank.

The guideline for the development and introduction of a framework for the management and control of operational risk should be the economic benefit in the form of cost savings through a reduction in the number and size of losses, optimisation of the measures for coping with risk (in particular the insurance programme) by means of business line-spanning communications, decision-making aids in the management environment of the whole bank and the improvement of protection against high-severity, low-frequency losses. Regulatory requirements should merely play the role of a boundary condition rather than be the driver.

Experience in the market and credit risk areas shows that decades may pass between the first steps in a new discipline and the presence of mature methods largely accepted in the marketplace. Seen from this point of view, the topic of operational risk has an interesting future in store. Dynamic development may be expected, due to the increasing number of financial institutions that are devoting themselves intensively to the development of such methods, and to isolated activities in the academic sphere as well.

Furthermore, it does not seem unlikely that, with the extension of the range of risks considered, the definition and delimitation of operational risk will change. Especially, reputational and strategic risks, but also business risks, are on the one hand increasingly being recognised as relevant, but on the other have potentially significant overlaps with operational risk.

This could lead to a shift in components from one risk type to another. As the difficulties in identifying and categorising operational risk show, some components are not particularly intuitive. Thus it is not implausible to remove certain components of external effects entirely from the definition of operational risk and to assign them to business risk. There is also no consensus up to now as to whether legal risks are a risk type of their own or a category, or are instead simply assimilated into the risks arising from processes, people, systems and external effects.

In the case of risk assessment instruments, there is on the one hand great euphoria on the part of those who are introducing them for the first time, and on the other not inconsiderable frustration on the part of those who are not able to recognise any changes on repeated execution, at least not any increased risk sensitivity. Risk indicators are often irresistibly relevant at first glance, at second glance difficult to determine and often lacking any statement concerning the development of existing or future risk. The same thing applies to indicators as to risk assessments, namely that only experience in their use can lead to an improvement in results and methods. Time is an essential factor; learning effects and adjustments to corporate culture are unavoidable.

Ideally, complete and error-free loss data would be available for all aspects of operational risk. This would, at least from the point of view of the quants, make the models considerably more stable and thus the determination of risk capital incomparably more precise. This ideal state of affairs will never be reached in reality, because the definition is too broad to enable a completely objective identification and evaluation to be made. However, the measure of despair should remain within narrow limits, as models are always only a simplified picture of reality; even in the case of complete data, the past holds only limited informative value for the future.

As in the case of market and credit risk, a quantification model for operational risk can only support management decisions, but can never make them obsolete. The creation of an appropriate organisational structure with clear assignment of tasks and responsibilities therefore always has priority over all models.

The existing processes and methodologies for the management and control of operational risk were developed over a short period, to some extent on the basis of knowledge from neighbouring disciplines. In the course of this, pragmatic solutions were worked out, in view of the limited resources. Naturally, there has been up to now on the one hand a lack of many years' experience with their application and on the other hand also a lack of an at least partial scientific foundation. It is to be hoped that both will be remedied in coming years.

It should be borne in mind that the area of operational risk has a markedly interdisciplinary character, because of its breadth and its intensive interrelation with the bank's organisation and its employees. In particular, the fact that operational risk can be associated in most cases with consciously or unconsciously incorrect human conduct leads to psychological considerations regarding the behaviour of bank employees becoming more important than mathematical models for the analysis of the relevant data.

A starting point for research could be the work of Daniel Kahnemann and Vernon Smith on the topic of decisions under uncertainty (prospect theory), which was honoured with a Nobel Prize in 2002. This impressively demonstrated from the psychological point of view that the assumption of a *Homo oeconomicus* is not tenable, in particular in the case of making decisions under risk. These findings have an influence on all components of the management and control of operational risk, but in particular on the risk assessment and scenario analysis methods.

Principal-agent models can also be of use in the analysis of the behaviour of employees and managers in the risk management process. Thus, the derivation of an incentive and remuneration system that supports virtually complete reporting and collection of loss data and objective risk evaluation by means of risk assessments and scenario analysis is conceivable.

Game-theory approaches can be employed in the matter of validating expert opinions. It is a question here of the best possible composition of workshops to answer such presentations of subjects within a business line and possibly spanning business lines.

Organisational theory can be useful in the development of a suitable management structure. Here, it is, among other things, a question of the role and hierarchical involvement of the decentralised persons responsible for operational risk management.

From the social sciences impulses can be expected for the best possible design of questionnaires, and from the engineering sciences ideas for scenario analysis.

The functionality of all these possibilities to optimise the methods of management and control must prove itself in practical application. The continuation of the open exchange conducted in the past between the parties involved concerning accumulated experience helps establish operational risk as a risk type having equal rights with the more established market and credit risks.

References

Alexander, C., (ed), 2003, *Operational Risk: Regulation, Analysis and Management* (London: FT Prentice Hall).

BBA/ISDA/RMA, 1999, *Operational Risk – The Next Frontier* (Philadelphia: Risk Management Association).

BIS, 1988, "International Convergence of Capital Measurement and Capital Standards", Bank for International Settlements, Basel.

BIS, 1998, "Operational risk management", Bank for International Settlements, Basel.

BIS, 1999, "A New Capital Adequacy Framework", Bank for International Settlements, Basel.

BIS, 2001a, "Consultative Document Operational Risk", supporting document to the New Basel Capital Accord, Bank for International Settlements, Basel.

BIS, 2001b, "Working Paper on the Regulatory Treatment of Operational Risk", Bank for International Settlements, Basel.

BIS, 2002a, "Sound Practices for the Management and Supervision of Operational Risk", Bank for International Settlements, Basel.

BIS, 2002b, "Quantitative Impact Study 3, Technical Guidance", Bank for International Settlements, Basel.

BIS, 2002c, "The Quantitative Impact Study for Operational Risk: Overview of Individual Loss Data and Lessons Learned", Bank for International Settlements, Basel.

BIS, 2003a, "Sound Practices for the Management and Supervision of Operational Risk", Bank for International Settlements, Basel.

BIS, 2003b, "Consultative Document The New Basel Capital Accord", Bank for International Settlements, Basel.

BIS, 2003c, "The Joint Forum – Operational Risk Transfer Across Financial Sectors", Bank for International Settlements, Basel.

BIS, 2003d, "The Joint Forum – Trends in Risk Integration and Aggregation", Bank for International Settlements, Basel.

BIS, 2004, "International Convergence of Capital Measurement and Capital Standards: A Revised Framework", Bank for International Settlements, Basel.

Brink, G. J. van den and T. Kaiser, 2004, "Operational Risk vs. Credit Risk: Similarities and Differences", *Operational Risk*, January.

Ceske, R., J. Hernandéz and L. Sánchez, 2000, "Quantifying Event Risk: The Next Convergence", *Journal of Risk Finance*, **1(3)**.

Cruz, M., 2002, *Modeling, Measuring and Hedging Operational Risk* (New York: Wiley).

Cruz, M. (ed), 2004, *Operational Risk Modelling and Analysis: Theory and Practice* (London: Risk Books).

Davis, E. (ed), 2005, *Operational Risk. Practical Approaches to Implementation* (London: Risk Books).

Doerig, H.-U., 2000, *Operational Risk in Financial Services – An Old Challenge in a New Environment*, Institut International d'Etudes Bancaires, Zurich.

Dowd, K., 1998, *Beyond Value at Risk: The New Science of Risk Management* (New York: Wiley).

EC, 1993, "Capital Adequacy of Investment Firms and Credit Institutions", Brussels.

EC, 1999, "A Review of Regulatory Capital Requirements for EU Credit Institutions and Investment Firms", Brussels.

EC, 2001, "Commission Services' Second Consultative Document on Review of Regulatory Capital for Credit Institutions and Investment Firms", Brussels.

EC, 2002, "Working Document of the Commission Services on Capital Requirements for Credit Institutions and Investment Firms", Brussels.

EC, 2003, "Commission Services' Third Consultative Document on Review of Regulatory Capital for Credit Institutions and Investment Firms", Brussels.

EC, 2004, "Re-casting Council Directive 93/6/EEC of 15th March, 1993 on the capital adequacy of investment firms and credit institutions", Brussels.

EC, 2006, "Directive 2006/49/EC of the European Parliament and of the Council of 14th June, 2006 on the capital adequacy of investment firms and credit institutions (recast)", Brussels.

Embrechts, P., C. Klüppelberg and T. Mikosch, 1997, *Modelling Extremal Events for Insurance and Finance* (Berlin: Springer).

***Euromoney*,** 1996, "Risk management's final frontier", *Euromoney*, September.

Frachot, A., P. Georges and T. Roncalli, 2001, *Loss-distribution approach for Operational Risk* (Paris: Manuscript).

Haas, M. and T. Kaiser, 2003, "Tackling the insufficiency of loss data for Op Risk quantification", *Operational Risk*, October.

Hoffman, D., 2002, *Managing Operational Risk* (New York: Wiley).

Kaiser, T. and M. Köhne, 2003, "Qualifying for Advanced Measurement Approaches: Operational Risk Sound Practices and Beyond", in *KPMG – Basel Briefing 3* (London: KPMG).

Kaiser, T. and M. Köhne, 2003, "Incentives for consistent operational risk management and reporting", in *KPMG – Basel Briefing 5* (London: KPMG).

Klugman, S., H. Panjer and G. Willmot, 1998, *Loss Models: From Data to Decisions* (New York: Wiley).

KPMG International, 2005a, "Basel II – A Worldwide Challenge for the Banking Business", Amsterdam.

KPMG International, 2005b, "Basel II – A Closer Look: Managing Operational Risk", Amsterdam.

Markowitz, H., 1952, "Portfolio Selection", *Journal of Finance*, **7**.

Marschall, C., 2000, *Measuring and Managing Operational Risk in Financial Institutions: Tools, Techniques, and other Resources* (New York: Wiley).

Moody's Investor Service, 2003, *Moody's Analytical Framework for Operational Risk* (London: Moody's).

Myers, G., 1996, "The Alternative Insurance Market: A Primer", *John Liner Review, Fall.*

Ong, M. (ed), 2004, *The Basel Handbook: A Guide for Financial Practitioners* (London: Risk Books).

Risk Books, (ed), 1998, *Operational Risk and Financial Institutions* (London: Risk Books).

Risk Books, (ed), 2003, *Advances in Operational Risk* (London: Risk Books).

Smith, C., 2002, "Providing cover for operational risk", *Banker*, October.

Index